Y0-AQU-268

Life on the Go

Devotional

for Moms

Inspiration From God for Busy Lifestyles

Life on the Go

D e v o t i o n a l

for Moms

Inspiration From God for Busy Lifestyles

By
Harrison House

Harrison House

Tulsa, Oklahoma

Unless otherwise noted, all Scripture quotations are taken from the *Holy Bible, New International Version®*. NIV®. Copyright © 1973, 1978, Zondervan Publishing House. All rights reserved.

Scripture quotations marked (NLT) are taken from the *Holy Bible, New Living Translation*, copyright © 1996. Used by permission of Tyndale House Publishers, Inc., Wheaton, Illinois 60189. All rights reserved.

Scripture quotations marked (AMP) are taken from *The Amplified Bible. Old Testament* copyright © 1965, 1987 by Zondervan Corporation, Grand Rapids, Michigan. *New Testament* copyright © 1958, 1987 by The Lockman Foundation, La Habra, California. Used by permission.

Scripture quotations marked (MESSAGE) are taken from *The Message*, copyright © by Eugene H. Peterson, 1993, 1994, 1995, 1996. Used by permission of NavPress Publishing Group.

Scripture quotations marked (NASB) are taken from the *New American Standard Bible®*. Copyright © 1960, 1962, 1963, 1968, 1971, 1972, 1973, 1975, 1977 by The Lockman Foundation. Used by permission. www.Lockman.org

Scripture quotations marked (NKJV) are taken from *The New King James Version*. Copyright © 1979, 1980, 1982, Thomas Nelson, Inc.

Scripture quotations marked (KJV) are taken from the *King James Version* of the Bible.

Unless otherwise noted, all devotions were written by Emily Steele.

10 09 08 07 06   10 9 8 7 6 5 4 3 2 1

Life on the Go for Moms:
Inspiration From God for Busy Lifestyles
ISBN 1-57794-683-9
Copyright © 2006 by Harrison House, Inc.

Published by Harrison House, Inc.
PO Box 35035
Tulsa, OK 74153

Printed in the United States of America. All rights reserved under International Copyright Law. Contents and/or cover may not be reproduced in whole or in part in any form without the written consent of the Publisher.

Contents

Introduction

Take a time-out, relax, and give your attention to the One who can give you powerful encouragement and great wisdom for your family. Your life may be moving fast, but when you find a few moments each day to let God influence your thoughts, your perspective will shift and those things that are weighing you down will begin to lift. Take this enriching inspiration with you and as pockets of time open up, give a little to God and see the difference it will make.

In God's House

> One thing I ask of the Lord, this is what I seek: that I may dwell in the house of the Lord all the days of my life, to gaze upon the beauty of the Lord and to seek him in his temple.
>
> Psalm 27:4

Your alarm clock sounds, and you roll over to turn it off. You recall the dirty laundry that is cascading over the top of the hamper, the children's papers and sneakers strewn across the floor, dishes on one side of the kitchen sink—and the plumber is scheduled to arrive in an hour to fix the garbage disposal.

You're tempted to roll over and just forget it all, but as you reach to press the snooze button your arm brushes a Book you've set there for moments like these. Its wisdom and peace beckon you, moving past the mental commotion to penetrate your spirit, which recognizes the priceless opportunity before you: a moment in God's presence. Thoughts of your earthly home and concerns vanish as you open the Book and find Him there.

David knew the agony of waking up to disarray and mental commotion. Yet, he wrote in Psalm 27:4 that all he wanted was to dwell in the presence of the Lord. While running for his life from King Saul, David spent many nights in caves and under the open desert sky. The one thing that kept him going was the thought of home—not the cave and not the palace, but the very presence of the Lord. Above everything in this world, David longed for time in God's house.

Do you long for time in God's house? Sometimes life can numb our minds to the longing of our spirits. The reason David's spirit pulled him so strongly toward God's house was that he knew from repeated experience the amazing benefits there. He knew God's house offered light, salvation, beauty, safety, exaltation, mercy, instruction, good-ness—and more. (See Ps. 27.)

Do you know what God's house has for you? Like David, you can receive the benefits of time in God's pres-ence. You can choose to dwell in God's house—every day. It's not that you'll neglect your earthly responsibilities. Contrarily, as you live in God's house on a continual basis, you'll find everything you need to perform all God has called you to do each day.

Before you roll over for five more minutes of sleep or dash out of bed to tackle all the disarray in your life, satisfy the longing of your spirit and find the strength in God to do whatever you have to do today. Grab the Book and get on your knees for some time in God's house. You'll be glad you did.

for Moms

Take a Break

Spend time in God's house today, and He will help you manage yours.

You Can Do This!

The Bible tells us many times, "Fear not," but motherhood often challenges our will to remain fearless. Do you remember when your toddler tried to run toward a busy street, when your grade-schooler went to summer camp for the first time, or when your teenager grabbed the keys and set out on his first solo car drive? Each time, something inside of you wanted to pull your child back into the shelter of your arms forever, safe from all harm.

> But now, this is what the Lord says—he who created you, O Jacob, he who formed you, O Israel: "Fear not, for I have redeemed you; I have summoned you by name; you are mine."
>
> Isaiah 43:1

And, all this time, weighing more heavily on you than the desire to keep your kids safe from physical harm has been the desire to protect them from emotional and spiritual harm. You were privileged to see them enter this world with pure minds and unbroken hearts, and you want that wholeness to remain. Yet the world they live in lures them toward impurity and slings arrows of pain and brokenness toward their hearts.

Then comes the question in your own heart: "Can I really do this? Can I be the mother God wants me to be for these children?"

In Isaiah 43:1, God speaks to His chosen people, "Fear not, for I have redeemed you; I have summoned you by name; you are mine." You are not only one of God's chosen, but you are His choice to be the mother of the children He has entrusted to your care. In the great, eternal plan of God, it is no accident that you are the mother of your children. God summoned you by name to mother them, and He says, "Fear not.... You are mine."

God did not lightly give you the calling to mother your children, and He has not left you empty-handed for the task. The equipment is within you and before you. Not only did He give you the natural instincts to nurture your children as they grow physically, but as a daughter of God you have His supernatural ability within you to rise above the limitations of this world and guide your children into wholeness of spirit, soul, and body. You also have access to the wisdom of His Word—the Bible—to guide you each step of the way.

Prayer

Lord, You know better than I the plans You have for each of my children, so teach me how to nurture them. In the difficult moments, thank You for holding me close and reassuring me that You have called and equipped me for the task. I will seek You daily for the strength and wisdom I need, in Jesus' name. Amen.

Raising Up God's Champions

Then I heard the voice of the Lord saying, "Whom shall I send? And who will go for us?" And I said, "Here am I. Send me!"

Isaiah 6:8

From Noah to Abraham to David and beyond, God has always been a champion builder. He looks at your kids and sees the same champion Spirit that was in them.

Several characteristics set God's champions apart. First, God's champions know His voice. Training our children to hear God's voice gives them a vital key to becoming His champions. Because God's spoken word in the heart is always confirmed in His written Word, our first step is to teach them His Word.

Second, God's champions believe His promise and follow His leading. Though no rain had ever fallen on earth in the history of humankind, Noah believed God would send a flood and built the ark. Though he was childless at one hundred years old, Abraham believed God would make him a father of many nations. Though a scrawny teenager, David believed God would use him to slay a giant and win a war for His people. Because of their unwavering faith, God won irrevocable victories through each of them.

Third, God's champions expect to win. First Corinthians 9:24 says, "Do you not know that in a race all the runners run, but only one gets the prize? Run in such a way as to get the prize." When your children learn—from the Word and from personal experience—that God is a winner, and all who follow Him are winners, His victory is the only thing they expect.

Fourth, God's champions understand that His anointing enables them to win. Psalm 23:5 in *The Amplified Bible* says, "You anoint my head with oil; my [brimming] cup runs over." When our children are anointed with the Holy Spirit for the tasks God gives them, they are empowered to win every time.

Finally, God's champions give Him all the glory. In Revelation 4:9-11 the apostle John saw that when we give God glory, the twenty-four elders fall down before Jesus and worship Him. Each of your children is marked as a champion who brings glory, honor, and power to God's name.

God calls out today, "Whom shall I send? And who will go for us?" Raise up your children to hear His voice, so that they can respond in unwavering faith, "Here am I. Send me!" (Isa. 6:8). Then get ready to see victory after victory won for God's kingdom through each one of your kids—His champions.

for Moms

Take a Break

Today, tell your kids about one of God's champions from His Word. Then tell them that they, too, are His champions.

In His Hands

Many people define themselves by what they do: "I'm a doctor," "I'm a receptionist," "I'm a mom," and so forth. We often place varying degrees of importance on each title and fight for a position at "the top." This doesn't apply just to entrepreneurs

> See, I have inscribed you on the palms of My hands; Your walls are continually before Me.
> Isaiah 49:16

and CEOs; we mothers can be among the fiercest competitors for a position at the top.

The truth is that we all want validation for what we do, and often motherhood can be a thankless job. While we're picking up the stray pieces of corn on the floor after our toddler's dinner, he isn't kneeling beside us saying, "Thanks, Mom!" More likely, he's pouring puzzle pieces all over his room! Or when we hear the car in the driveway at midnight and greet our teenager after sitting up worried, she doesn't say, "Thanks, Mom!" She walks briskly to her room, hoping to avoid our questions.

Yes, motherhood is often a thankless job—if we're looking for verbal thanks. And, yes, we can and should train our kids to say, "Thank you." But as wonderful as their gratitude may be, it can only give us a temporary boost to continue with the enormous task of motherhood. What we really need is something that is only available from heaven.

The Bible says that we are not to work for the applause of human beings, but for God alone. Jesus said, "Be careful not to do your 'acts of righteousness' before men, to be seen by them. If you do, you will have no reward from your Father in heaven" (Matt. 6:1). The reward from our Father in heaven is of much more value than the temporary reward of human recognition.

Our heavenly reward is, in part, the satisfaction of knowing that God is pleased with us not just for what we do, but for who we are. We are not the titles we may give ourselves—doctor, receptionist, or mom—we are more than these. We are His. When we realize this, we will walk in His peace.

We are not defined by what we do as mothers, as businesswomen, or as anything else, but by our relationship with God. Understanding this truth keeps us steady, even after our children have left home. Knowing we are His, we no longer strive for a place at the elusive top. We realize that we are already right where we need to be—in His hands.

Take a Break

Locate some Scriptures that define you as God sees you. For example, see Deuteronomy 28:1-14; Isaiah 43:1; 2 Corinthians 2:14; and Ephesians 5:1.

What's Inside?

> Tell those who are rich in this world not to be proud and not to trust in their money, which will soon be gone. But their trust should be in the living God, who richly gives us all we need for our enjoyment.
>
> I Timothy 6:17 NLT

We've all watched a commercial, seen an advertisement, or walked through the mall and have been caught up in our outward appearance. We think, *My jeans don't fit right...I need a manicure...I could really use some new shoes... I need to work out!* If we don't stop ourselves, we can get lost in other outward concerns—cars, houses, computers, savings accounts, retirement funds, and every other material thing.

God certainly desires to bless His children with the materials necessary to enjoy life. (See I Tim. 6:17.) However, He never intended for those things to be our focus. Jesus specifically said in Matthew 6:31-33 that we should not worry about what we will eat, drink, or wear because the Father knows what we need. We are to seek His kingdom and righteousness, and He will see to it that we have everything we need.

The New Testament apostles focused mostly on giving material possessions away. First John 3:17 says, "If anyone has material possessions and sees his brother in need but has no pity on him, how can the love of God be in him?"

Many people have worked so hard for every penny in their possession that they start to cling to their material wealth. Although they leaned on God through the penniless days, they tend to forget Him during days of plenty. In Deuteronomy 8:17-18 God warned Israel to always remember that He gave them the power to get the wealth they enjoyed.

Today, remember that God is the One who gives you the power to gain wealth, and ask Him to show you what He wants you to do with it. It's wonderful to have nice things and to be able to provide for our families, but what is most important is what is inside of us. First Peter 3:3-4 MESSAGE tells us, "Cultivate inner beauty, the gentle, gracious kind that God delights in."

Next time your outward needs holler for your attention, allow your spirit to refocus your attention on what really matters: Jesus in you. Seek Him and His righteousness and watch how His kingdom overtakes your life and meets every need.

Prayer

Lord, thank You for being my provider. I seek You and Your righteousness first in my life, and I trust You to supply all my needs. Thank You for Your wisdom and ability to acquire and distribute material things to our family and those to whom You lead us to give, in Jesus' name. Amen.

The Gift We Give Back

Children are a gift from the
Lord, and we are privileged as
parents to present them back to
Him. As we train our children in His
ways, leading them into His presence, they become beautiful vessels
for His use.

> Children are a
> gift from the Lord;
> they are a reward
> from him.
> Psalm 127:3 NLT

A mother's opportunity to encourage her child's spiritual connection to the Father begins at conception. A
baby in the womb can hear noises from the outside world
and move to the rhythm of his mother's speech.[1] If his
physical body can receive (through hearing) and respond
(with motion) to the sounds around him, how much more
can his spirit receive and respond to the surrounding
spiritual environment?

The Bible promises us that when we gather together
in Jesus' name, He is in our midst. (Matt. 18:20.) Jesus'
presence heals, restores, saves, and matures every person
who spends time with Him. From the womb to high
school graduation and beyond, your child will benefit from
time in God's presence.

Speak Scriptures to your baby in your womb. Toddlers can memorize Scripture, especially when it is reinforced with motions or music. In fact, a child will learn any new biblical concept best when it reaches several of his senses—hearing, touch, sight, smell, and taste. That's why teaching tools like music, rhythm and rhyme, body movement, pictures, and object lessons, such as communion, are so effective.

God tells us, "Fix these words of mine in your hearts and minds; tie them as symbols on your hands and bind them on your foreheads" (Deut. 11:18). Today we can "bind" a symbol of God's Word to our kids with a sticker, a T-shirt, or a piece of jewelry that they carry on their person all day, reminding them of the biblical truths they have learned.

Through the creative use of visual aids in our homes, we can deeply instill God's Word in our children. Colossians 1:28 summarizes our ultimate goal in teaching our children:

> We warn them and teach them with all the wisdom God has given us, for we want to present them to God, perfect [or *mature*] in their relationship to Christ.

As we lovingly feed our children God's Word, their sense of identity and purpose grows. They become mature in their relationship with Jesus. Then we are privileged to give back to Him the precious gifts He gave us.

Take a Break

If your family doesn't presently share a consistent daily devotional time, initiate one today.

Let Him Love Through You

May he be enthroned in God's presence forever; appoint your love and faithfulness to protect him.

Psalm 61:7

In 1 Corinthians 12 Paul tells us that the body of Christ is composed of many members, each operating in a significant function. At the end of the chapter, however, Paul concludes that one function is more significant than any of these. It is love.

No matter what your gift and calling may be, you are called and equipped to love, and this is particularly true for mothers. Our bodies are designed to nurture children from conception and after birth during breast-feeding. Without our affection and nurture, our children will not flourish. Every child needs love.

As we nurture our children with love, we begin to see love reflected back to us. The principle of sowing and reaping is constantly at work in our relationship with our children. If love is what we desire to reap from our children's lives, we need to make sure that love is what we sow into them.

We need to know what love is and what it is not. For example, love is not silently submitting to whatever our children do or whatever is done to them. Love is taking an active role in their lives, guarding them with and imparting to them the nature of their heavenly Father.

Love is not passive but active. It is not weak but strong. The strength of love can be seen in 1 Corinthians 13:7 and Psalm 61:7, which both identify love as a protector. Love is *everything* that God is because God is love. This is what our children need, and this is what we can give them.

Yes, we will make mistakes. God knew we would, and He also knew that His grace would be sufficient for us. If we depend on Him, His love will shine through our lives and be reflected back to us through our children's lives. We can depend on it, because His love never fails.

Prayer

Father, in Jesus' name, I thank You for loving my children through me today. I have all the attributes of love inside because I am a participant in Your nature. I am patient and kind. I do not envy or boast. I am not proud, rude, self-seeking, or easily angered. I keep no record of wrongs. I do not delight in evil but rejoice with the truth. I always protect, always trust, always hope, always persevere. Your love working in and through me never fails. Amen.

Go for It

> Delight yourself in the Lord and he will give you the desires of your heart.
> Psalm 37:4

So many times in life, we think, *Oh, if only I had time to do this,* or *If only I could have that.* And, though the thought comes to us repeatedly, we never do anything to fulfill that desire.

Let's say you've been thinking, *I need to spend some quiet time with God every day,* or *I would really like to start a business,* or *I wish I could play tennis.* Whatever your desire, if it's something you haven't yet accomplished, then you've probably considered a million reasons why you can't have what you want.

It happens to all of us, and as mothers our desires often come last on our priority lists. However, if we are to live the fulfilled and meaningful lives God desires for us, we can't just shrug off our desires. What we need to do is evaluate them to see whether they're worth our attention and effort to attain. Our first question should be, "Is this something God wants for me?"

Often, God is the One who plants desires in our hearts, sometimes for a purpose we cannot readily see. Psalm 37:4 says, "Delight yourself in the Lord and he will give you the desires of your heart." If you believe God has planted a desire in your heart, ask Him to help you fulfill that desire.

God plants desires in your heart, and He can fulfill them—when you press toward Him. Psalm 20:4 says, "May he give you the desire of your heart and make all your plans succeed." When you make plans to attain the desire He has given you, He will make your plans succeed.

God has good things in store for you. Today, commit to follow Him step by step into His ultimate plan. Start with one desire, and write it down. In Habakkuk 2:2, the Lord told the prophet, "Write the vision and make it plain on tablets, that he may run who reads it."

What vision has God given you? You are endowed with a unique purpose, and in order to fulfill that purpose you will need to press toward the desires God has given you. They may seem trivial, or they may seem unattainable, but don't neglect to reach for them as He leads you. One step in the right direction could catapult you into the next level of the calling on your life. Take a risk, and you'll realize it's no risk at all—because all of heaven backs you when you reach for God's desires.

Take a Break

Write down your God-given vision, and take one step toward it today.

Time With God in a Busy Schedule

> Impress them on your children. Talk about them when you sit at home and when you walk along the road, when you lie down and when you get up.
>
> Deuteronomy 6:7

With church, school, sports, clubs, lessons, and a flurry of other activities, our kids' lives can become very time-constrained. Nevertheless, we need to help them make room in their busy schedules for God. However, sometimes we don't see the opportunities to imprint His Word on their hearts.

In this passage in Deuteronomy, God clearly identifies those opportunities: "Talk about them when you sit at home and when you walk along the road, when you lie down and when you get up" (v. 7). In other words, every time we're with our kids—in the living room, in the car, at the table, and so forth—we should talk with them about God's Word.

God requires us to help our kids maintain a relationship with Him. Even when our schedules are busy, we can do that by establishing a relationship with our kids that invites their questions and their insights about God. By our example and through our conversations, we can encourage them to remain in His presence all day, every day.

Psalm 91:1 and 9 speak of making God our shelter, our dwelling, and our refuge. We can teach our children to live their lives in continual fellowship with Him. One form of ongoing fellowship with God is praise. Psalm 34:1 NKJV says, "I will bless the Lord at all times; His praise shall continually be in my mouth." With music or with simple words of thanks to God, our kids can learn to live in His presence.

Another form of perpetual interaction with God is prayer. First Thessalonians 5:17 says, "Pray without ceasing." When we make prayer an ongoing part of our lives, we can help our children see the necessity and the benefits of daily communion with Him.

Whether we have five minutes or five hours with our kids, we can bring God's Word into our conversation and help them build their relationship with Him. When we remain alert to the opportunities God so clearly pointed out to us so many years ago, we give our children the priceless gift of a vibrant relationship with Him.

Prayer

Father, in Jesus' name, I thank You for all the opportunities You've given me to teach my children Your Word. Holy Spirit, enlighten their minds as they hear Your Word, and fill my mouth

*with the truth that they need. Remind us as a family to contin-
ually commune with You, in Jesus' name. Amen.*

Another Good Day

If we're honest, we'll admit that not every dawn elicits a smile and a cry of rejoicing from us. Whether we have gotten too little sleep, we're in pain, or we have a task ahead of us that we'd rather avoid, we are sometimes tempted to think, *Looks like it's going to be another one of those days.*

But we must take issue with that thought. Our expectation determines our attitude, which determines our experience. If we expect a bad day, then we will have a bad day. The truth is, in Jesus there are no bad days. Whatever we face, He is there to work all things for our good. (Rom. 8:28.)

> The stone which the builders rejected has become the chief cornerstone. This is from the Lord and is His doing; it is marvelous in our eyes. This is the day which the Lord has brought about; we will rejoice and be glad in it.
>
> Psalm 118:22-24
> AMP

Today, remember that you live in the day of salvation, the day of grace, the day of provision, the day of healing. You live in the day that was purchased for you two thousand years ago when your God gave His life for your redemption.

for Moms

Jesus was the stone that the builders rejected, the One whose sacrifice purchased this day of God's favor for you. Paul also writes of this day, quoting the prophet Isaiah:

> For he says, "In the time of my favor I heard you, and in the day of salvation I helped you." I tell you, now is the time of God's favor, now is the day of salvation.
>
> 2 Corinthians 6:2

Every day since the Atonement, Jesus' purchase of our salvation, we have been given a reason to rejoice and be glad. Today is the day of salvation! Therefore, on this day of grace, freedom, and joy, praise God for your salvation and deliverance. His mercy and lovingkindness endure forever—they extend even to today. No matter what last night looked like, and regardless of what lies ahead, rejoice in today! What a good gift it is!

Prayer

Jesus, I praise You, my Salvation and my Redeemer! I will not be downcast; I put my hope in You, my Savior and my God. (Ps. 42:5.) I speak of Your righteousness and my mouth is filled with Your praise, declaring Your splendor all day long. (Ps. 35:28; 71:8.) I will lead my family in boasting of You all day, and we will praise Your name forever. (Ps. 44:8.) In Jesus' name, I rejoice and am glad in this day that You, my Lord, made! Thank You for it, Lord! Amen.

Hold On Tight

Do you remember the days when you first fell in love with your husband? The tingling excitement when you caught his eye from across the room? The first time you held his hand? That momentous first kiss? Now that you've caught this man—the object of your desire—will you hold on to him?

> When I found him whom my soul loves; I held on to him and would not let him go.
>
> Song of Solomon 3:4 NASB

Sometimes the demands of motherhood and life in general can distract us from the passion we once felt for our husbands. We are so drained from chasing our children that we are too tired to even remember the comfort of our husbands' embrace.

While our children certainly need our loving attention, we must realize that they also need their parents to love each other. Our loving relationship gives them security, demonstrates the love God wants them to have in marriage, and shows them the love Jesus has for the church. (Eph. 5:22-33.)

For the sake of your children, and for the sake of your marriage, remember the chase and hold on to your prize. Once in a while, put down the dishes, the laundry, and even the children to rediscover the man with whom you fell in love. Learn about his interests and enjoy them with him. Tell him your dreams and let him help you reach them.

Remember the words of Solomon, who told his son, "...may you rejoice in the wife of your youth" (Prov. 5:18). Rejoice in the husband of your youth. Years of marriage and parenthood shouldn't diminish the joy you find in your husband. Rather, it should enhance it because you have been given the opportunity to share the life you could only dream of then.

Whether or not your life today is what you imagined it would be, don't stop dreaming now. You have a full life of shared opportunities ahead of you. Commit to staying unified with your husband in every way so that you can accomplish everything for which God united you, and show your children the joy in your life together.

Prayer

Father, thank You for the gift of my husband. I speak blessings upon him today, in the name of Jesus. Teach me and my husband how to communicate and meet one another's needs and love each other more deeply every day. I choose to chase my husband, just as I did in the days of our youth. I plead the blood of Jesus over our marriage, and I declare that it is vibrant and strong—a vivid example for our children to follow in their future marriages. I am committed to my marriage vows, and I will follow You in fulfilling them, in Jesus' name. Amen.

Make an Eternal Impact

No discipline seems pleasant at the time, but painful. Later on, however, it produces a harvest of right-eousness and peace for those who have been trained by it.

Hebrews 12:11

Disciplining our children isn't easy, but it is necessary in order for them to prosper and be successful in God's plan for their lives. Godly parental discipline introduces them to the concept of right and wrong choices, and it steers them toward doing what is right.

It's important to offer children opportunities to make good choices. Remember: God empowered Adam and Eve to make decisions when He told them they could eat of any tree in the Garden. However, He clearly identified the boundaries.

"You are free to eat from any tree in the garden; but you must not eat from the tree of the knowledge of good and evil, for when you eat of it you will surely die."

Genesis 2:16,17

God understood the dangers that threatened His creation. He knew the serpent's rebellious influence, so He gave Adam and Eve a clear directive in order to protect them from harm. In the same way, we know of the dangers that lurk in this world and are aware of the problems that can result from making bad choices. Therefore, we offer our children good choices, set boundaries, define consequences, and enforce rules. This gives them a safe environment in which to grow.

In a nutshell, discipline is an expression of love. Proverbs 3:12 says, "The Lord disciplines those he loves, as a father the son he delights in." We discipline our children with the intent to keep them safe from harm and to empower them to live the satisfying lives that God intended for them—the lives we want for them because we love them.

Following God's example, we should always be motivated by love. Our children's happiness can only be achieved by adherence to God's principles, so we must base our parenting structure on His Word. Proverbs 22:6 NLT says, "Teach your children to choose the right path, and when they are older, they will remain upon it." As soon as our children learn to choose that path for themselves, they become a blessing to future generations as well. Today, let's accept our responsibility and set our children on a course toward blessing forever.

Take a Break

Write out a discipline plan for your household. Then schedule a family meeting to clearly communicate the plan.

In His Strength

Acts 1:8 tells us that when the Holy Spirit comes into our lives, so does His power, strength, and ability. And the end of Acts 1:8 tells us that His power, strength, and ability are to enable us to be witnesses of Jesus wherever we go.

As mothers, our greatest influence on the world starts at home. We must rely on the strength of the Holy Spirit within to do all God has called us to do. At some point our human energy and ability will run out, but God's never will!

> But ye shall receive power, after that the Holy Ghost is come upon you: and ye shall be witnesses unto me both in Jerusalem, and in all Judaea, and in Samaria, and unto the uttermost part of the earth.
>
> Acts 1:8

When we allow the Holy Spirit to work in and through us, we are no longer limited to the power of the physical body or the physical mind. We rise to a supernatural level of ability and strength—God's ability and strength. In Colossians 1:29 AMP, Paul speaks of this "...superhuman energy which He so mightily enkindles and works within me." As moms, we need superhuman energy—and we can have it every day!

for Moms

44

Paul's words to Timothy recorded in 2 Timothy 1:5-7 AMP remind us to live aware of the power of God's Spirit within. We are told that by faith, we lean our entire personality on Him in absolute trust in His power. (See 1 Tim. 1:5 AMP.) We are encouraged to stir up the gift of God that is in us (v. 6) and that we do not have a spirit of fear but of power, love, and a well-balanced and disciplined mind (v. 7).

When we lean on the Holy Spirit, we are invested with His power, love, and calm and well-balanced mind and discipline and self-control. Imagine how effective we would be as moms if we were to "stir up...the gift of God, [the inner fire]" and demonstrate His character every day!

The way we stir up that inner fire is by spending time in His presence, magnifying Him through our words of praise, speaking His Word, and praying in the Spirit. Jude tells us that when we pray in the Holy Spirit, we build ourselves up in faith. (Jude 1:20.) Stirring up the gift of the Holy Spirit within enables us to rise above the challenges of this world and to be the mothers He has called us to be.

Prayer

Heavenly Father, in the name of Jesus, I praise You! I receive Your gift of the Holy Spirit. I thank You that with Him comes all of Your power, strength, and ability; Your love and Your sound mind. I pray in the Spirit to build myself up. (Jude 1:20.) Thank You, Lord, for ministering through me today. Amen.

When Dad Is Gone

> A father of the fatherless, a defender of widows, is God in His holy habitation. God sets the solitary in families.
>
> Psalm 68:5,6 NKJV

Parenting is a demanding job for anyone, but when a mom is left to care for her children without the support or the presence of their father it can feel like an overwhelming burden. Single moms, God wants you to know that you are not alone in rearing your children. He is with you, and He holds a special place in His heart for your family.

Psalm 68:5 says that your children have a Father—the faithful, loving, powerful, and merciful God. He wants to father them, and He wants you to help them know Him better. Psalm 68:5 also says that He is the defender of widows. Regardless of the reason for your husband's absence, God wants to be your defender, your protector.

God will cover you with His wings, where you will find shelter and confidence every day. (Ps. 57:1.) No evil will be able to touch you or your children when you abide in Him, and no sickness or tragedy will be allowed under His covering over you. (Ps. 91:10.)

Psalm 68:6 says that God wants to set the solitary in families. If you feel alone, take every opportunity to surround your family with trustworthy people who are genuinely committed to God and to fulfilling His purpose—and these will become your partners in faith and victory.

The Bible reveals what God can do for your family when you trust Him: "He hath delivered my soul in peace from the battle that was against me: for there were many with me" (Ps. 55:18 KJV). The word "peace" here is the Hebrew word *shalom,* which indicates wholeness—nothing missing or broken. No matter what battles rage against you, God can make your family whole.

By no means are you or your children alone. Just as a great host of heavenly warriors protected Elisha and his servant from an army of thousands, a great heavenly host surrounds you and your children. (2 Kings 6.) Those who are with you are more than those who oppose you. (v. 16.)

Today, trust God to be the Father to your children, to protect you, and to give you a family of faith. Trust Him to meet every need in your lives. Ask Him to reveal Himself so clearly to you and your children that you live assured of His presence, His protection, His help, His provision, and His love.

for Moms

Take a Break

Meditate on God's ability to protect you and to be a Father to your children. Remind your children of His love today.

Our Children's Faith

It's something we'd probably rather not think about—the idea that our children may one day, or may even now, have doubts about the Christian faith. The philosophies of this world lure them every which way but heavenward; and even if we choose to shelter them, our influence can only reach so far.

> Knowing that your faith is alive keeps us alive.
>
> I Thessalonians 3:8 MESSAGE

Our heavenly Father continues to speak to us as He spoke to the Israelites: "This day I call heaven and earth as witnesses against you that I have set before you life and death, blessings and curses. Now choose life, so that you and your children may live" (Deut. 30:19). Because He longs for our blessing and our children's blessing, He urges us, "Choose life."

Unfortunately, neither God nor we can choose life for our children. How we choose influences our kids. When we believe God's Word and live what we believe, their lives are impacted for good. But faith is an action that requires choice. Hebrews 11:1 says, "Now faith is being sure of what we hope for and certain of what we do not see." We can't make our children have faith. They must do that for themselves.

for Moms

Certainly, we are not required to sit passively by. In Deuteronomy 6:6-7 God commands us to instruct them in the truth all day, every day. By our words and actions, we are to train our children in the way they should go—that is, in the Word of God. Nonetheless, they must ultimately choose God for themselves.

The New Testament apostles lived and died to give people truth. To them true living came when they heard that their teaching had been effective—that the people they had taught continued to choose life. Consider the joy Paul must have felt when he heard from prison "good news about your faith" (v. 6). Suddenly, everything he had suffered became weightless: "For now we really live," he wrote, "since you are standing firm in the Lord" (v. 7).

Like the New Testament apostles, we want to truly live, knowing our children continue to choose life. Therefore, we must give our children sound instruction; we must give them the Word. Then we must be confident in that Word to work in them. Speak the Word, live it, pray it, and then trust it to do all that God has sent it forth to do—producing for your children the fruit of eternal life.

Take a Break

In everything you do and say, encourage your kids to choose life.

Have a Talk With Dad

Prayer is our connection with our eternal Dad. When Jesus walked the earth, He lived a life of prayer. He took every opportunity to find a place of refuge and talk to His Father. Jesus came to the earth to guide and lead others, yet He often slipped away from His closest companions to recharge and refocus in the presence of His Father.

> Pray like this: Our Father in heaven, may your name be honored.
> Matthew 6:9 NLT

We too are here to guide and lead others—beginning with our children. Just as Jesus took time away from His followers to be replenished in the presence of the Father, so must we. If we want to impact our children for good, we cannot continually give of ourselves and never allow heaven to refresh and renew us.

We cannot ignore our needs or meet them ourselves. When Jesus had a need, He didn't just stifle it or fix it Himself. He taught us by example how to depend on the Father. When He had a need, He talked to His Father about it. So we must talk with our heavenly Father and receive all that we need as well.

for Moms

Jesus also taught us how to pray. Prayer is an immense privilege and responsibility that we must not take for granted, and we must teach our children that they can have a real connection with their heavenly Dad through prayer. When they need counsel, healing, favor, or provision, they can go to Him.

Prayer is our opportunity to communicate with our all-powerful Dad, and His power effects change in our world through the words we speak. Jesus taught us the power of the prayer of faith when He said, "Have faith in God....if anyone says to this mountain, 'Go, throw yourself into the sea,' and does not doubt in his heart but believes that what he says will happen, it will be done for him" (Mark 11:22,23). Natural circumstances must submit to the spoken Word of God.

Let's follow Jesus' example and spend time with our heavenly Dad so that we can know and do and speak His will on the earth, and so that we can teach our children to do the same.

Prayer

Father, I love speaking with You. You are everything I need, and I rest in You now. Teach me Your will so I can do what You want me to do and speak what You want me to speak so that Your will is done here on earth—in my life, in my home, and everywhere I go in prayer—as it is in heaven. Teach me and my children to depend on You daily for everything we need, in Jesus' name. Amen.

The Weapon That Conquers Fear

There is no fear in love. But perfect love drives out fear.

1 John 4:18

God wants us to have an abundant life. Jesus said, "The thief does not come except to steal, and to kill, and to destroy. I have come that they may have life, and that they may have it more abundantly" (John 10:10 NKJV). The enemy's ultimate target is our faith because our faith overcomes him:

> For whatever is born of God overcomes the world. And this is the victory that has overcome the world—our faith.
>
> 1 John 5:4 NKJV

Because the devil wants to conquer our faith, he has developed a tool that has disarmed people of every age, race, and gender. That tool is fear. Second Timothy tells us that "God has not given us a spirit of fear, but of power and of love and of a sound mind." Fear is a spirit, and it is not a gift from God. It is a weapon sent against us from the enemy. James 4:7 says, "Submit yourselves, then, to God. Resist the devil, and he will flee from you." When we resist the demonic spirit of fear, it has to flee!

In opposition to the fear that the devil tries to defeat us with, God has given us a spirit of "power, love, and a sound mind." That Spirit is the Holy Spirit, and He resides within us and has given us all of His attributes. We have His power. Jesus promised we would receive power when the Holy Spirit came upon us" (Acts 1:8 NKJV).

First John 4:18 focuses on one of these attributes as the invincible weapon against fear. It says, "There is no fear in love. But perfect love drives out fear." Ten verses before, in 1 John 4:8, we read that God is love. In order to conquer fear in our lives, we need true love: God Himself.

Perhaps 1 Corinthians 13:8 illustrates Love's power best: "Love never fails." Love never stops for any reason. It always was, always is, and always will be. It is completely unchanging and unconquerable, because it is God Himself. This love that cannot be stopped is the weapon that conquers fear. Abide in the presence of Love Himself and watch fear melt away.

Prayer

Father, in Jesus' name I thank You for the opportunity to know You through Your Son. You are love, and nothing can stand against You. In Jesus' name, and by the power of His blood, I resist the spirit of fear that would try to come against me or my family members. Holy Spirit, I welcome You and thank You that You fill each of us with Your power, love, and sound mind. Amen.

Becoming Spirit-Minded

So we make it our goal to please him, whether we are at home in the body or away from it.

2 Corinthians 5:9

We live in a very physically minded world that portrays men and women in top physical condition. As a result, many teens and adults struggle with eating disorders or have plastic surgery to try to improve their self-image.

As believers we know that physicality is not the most important aspect of our lives. The body is the least important because it depends on the soul and spirit to function. Knowing this, we need to focus on our spirits so that our children can see us properly valuing each part of our being.

The human body is the Master's design, and it truly is a masterpiece. Psalm 139:14 says, "I praise you because I am fearfully and wonderfully made." When God beholds each one of us He sees flawless beauty, and His perspective is what should shape our own and our children's.

We cannot neglect the body that He gave us because good health is essential to living long, satisfying lives. This is the desire of our Father: "With long life will I satisfy him and show him my salvation" (Ps. 91:16). Therefore, maintaining our physical health through exercise, nutrition, and rest is working hand-in-hand with God's will. However, in verse 14 God promises this long, satisfied life to those who love Him and acknowledge His name. The life of the spirit plays a vital role in the quality of the life of the body.

In a time when the flesh is glorified above the spirit, we would do well to direct our children's focus back to what really matters. This focus-shift must begin with our dedication to making the spirit within us the director of our lives. The apostle Paul wrote, "We make it our goal to please him, whether we are at home in the body or away from it" (2 Cor. 5:9). When our spirit directs our body's actions, we please the Father.

Paul also says, "Do you not know that your body is a temple of the Holy Spirit, who is in you, whom you have received from God? You are not your own" (1 Cor. 6:19). Our body is important because it is a vehicle by which the Holy Spirit moves in the earth today.

Give your children a strong example of one who glorifies Him in body so that they will see the good fruit of a spirit-driven life.

Take a Break

How can you strengthen each part of your being today—spirit, soul, and body?

Open the Door

God has a special purpose for each of your children, and He chose you to be a guide for them along their path to reaching the full potential He has placed within them. Everything about you—everything you have become and everything He has equipped you to be—can benefit

> He will turn the hearts of the fathers to their children, and the hearts of the children to their fathers.
> Malachi 4:6

your children. But communication must be open for these gifts to be passed to them.

Not only do you have gifts to give them, but they have gifts to give you. When you train them in the Bible and when they have the Spirit of God residing within, your children become mouthpieces of God's wisdom. Don't close the door on that possibility!

Don't allow fear or pride or anything else to barricade the door of communication between you and your children. God wants to deliver many gifts to you and to your children through that door. He wants to give you a healthy and joyful relationship with each other.

Luke 1:17 tells us that John the Baptist went "on before the Lord, in the spirit and power of Elijah, to turn the hearts of the fathers to their children and the disobedient to the wisdom of the righteous—to make ready a people prepared for the Lord." He prepared the hearts of the people for Christ's coming by ministering to unite families.

Christ is coming again, and to be prepared our hearts need to be toward each other in the home. The Father's desire is harmony in the home, and He requires that it be found according to His Word. Children are to "obey" their "parents in the Lord," meaning parents are to regulate their children's lives by God's Word. (Eph. 6:1 NKJV.) Parents are not to "provoke [their] children to wrath, but bring them up in the training and admonition of the Lord" (v. 4 NKJV). In short, God's way is the only way to have true harmony in the home.

Open the door of communication between yourself and your children by opening the door to God's Word in your family. God waits for the door to open so that He can bless your home. Break down the barriers, and get ready to give and receive all the gifts God has for your family.

Take a Break

With a hug, a note, or a word, open the door of communication with each of your children today.

Provision for Your Family

God is, has always been, and will always be the best financier. He wants us and our children to be secure in Him so that He can make our finances secure. Matthew 6:33 KJV says, "But seek ye first the kingdom of God, and his righteousness; and all these things shall be added unto you." When His kingdom is our focus, He provides everything we need on earth.

> I was young and now I am old, yet I have never seen the righteous forsaken or their children begging bread. They are always generous and lend freely; their children will be blessed.
>
> Psalm 37:25,26

The primary financial principle we learn from God's Word is that we will reap what we sow. In other words, when we give something of our substance (a seed), we receive multiplied times what we have sown (a harvest).

> You will be made rich in every way so that you can be generous on every occasion, and through us your generosity will result in thanksgiving to God.
>
> 2 Corinthians 9:11

God wants to give us everything we need and more so that we can give to those around us in need. It starts with our willingness to part with the seed that is in our hands. It may not look like much, but in God's economy that little seed can multiply and become more than enough to provide for our families and bless the people around us.

God sees our need, and He sees our children's needs, and He will always provide for them when we trust Him. He has provided all that we need to live an abundant life and doesn't want us to lack any good thing. (Psalm 84:11.) So when we look at our children, we must remember that they are first and foremost their heavenly Father's. As we surrender them to Him in prayer, we will see Him take care of them.

God has given us and our families the key to unlock His storehouse of provision. It is His Word. When we read it, believe it, speak it, and live it, we will see His blessings poured out on our families. We will see that God is everything He promised He would be—when we take Him at His Word.

Prayer

Father, in Jesus' name, I seek Your kingdom today. As I look in Your Word, I see that it is Your will to provide for my family. I recognize the seeds You have placed in our hands, and I thank You that as we plant them they become a bountiful harvest for us to enjoy and to give. I am a cheerful giver, Father, and I am glad to be Your blessed daughter! Amen.

for Moms

Stay Open
by Julie Lechlider

"My thoughts are completely different from yours," says the Lord. "And my ways are far beyond anything you could imagine. For just as the heavens are higher than the earth, so are my ways higher than your ways and my thoughts higher than your thoughts."
Isaiah 55:8,9 NLT

After two and a half years, Scott and I were excited to move back to our hometown with our young family. However, the house we moved into was more expensive than the house we had sold, so it was certain that I would have to return to work.

One cold December morning, after I saw my husband off to work, one daughter off to school, and the other down for her morning nap, I sat down in front of the crackling fireplace with my yellow highlighter to wade my way through the classified ads, looking for a new career.

After a long morning of dead-end phone calls, I was beginning to get frustrated. The phone rang and I answered it, hoping it was someone calling to set up an interview, but it was only my uncle who had just called to chat. My uncle was not walking with God and wasn't really open to hearing about the gospel, so I did not expect him to give me any real encouragement. After I explained what I was doing, he suggested that I contact a company I had worked for before we moved. I was strongly opposed to it—I had been there and done that and was ready for something new. However, after I hung up the phone the words kept coming back to me—the feeling just wouldn't go away. Later that afternoon, I decided to call an old friend that was still employed there just to see how things were going. After we talked for a few minutes and I told her that I was job hunting, she exclaimed that she had just been talking about me that same day because they were looking for someone to fill my old position and she had heard that I was back in town. By the end of that week I had been hired, and I was offered more money than I actually needed to make!

That was over four years ago, and today I know deep in my heart that God called me to the position I now hold at the company. I love what I do, and I have flexible work hours that allow me to be home for my daughters after school and to take care of my family. I have the best of both worlds. It scares me to think where I might be today had I not obeyed what God was telling me to do—and He gave me direction through the most unlikely person.

Take a Break

God works in ways we do not expect—so stay open. Trust God, no matter how unusual His ways look.

No Shame

The two of them, the Man and his Wife, were naked, but they felt no shame.

Genesis 2:25
MESSAGE

In the Garden of Eden before sin entered the world, man and woman lived together "without shame." Eve respected herself and her husband. Adam respected himself and his wife. God made them to be unique, and despite their differences they were completely comfortable in one another's presence. Neither felt shame in self, and neither felt shame in the other. However, the moment sin entered the world that mutual respect was lost.

At that moment, their eyes were opened, and they suddenly felt shame at their nakedness.

Genesis 3:7 NLT

The Bible calls Satan our accuser. (See Rev. 12:10.) When Adam and Eve believed his lie and sinned, they welcomed his accusations into their lives. In their fallen state, they felt shame in themselves and in one another.

Since that time, the enemy has continued to whisper accusations through people, who have unwittingly become his critical, condemning voice against themselves and others. The result is disrespect for God's creation and even for God.

At the cross Jesus confronted our accuser and His— and He overcame him! Colossians 2:15 says, "Having disarmed principalities and powers, He made a public spectacle of them, triumphing over them in it." Today, the accuser is defeated. He has no power over believers who walk in His authority. Still he has yet to be "hurled down." For this reason, I Peter 5:8 warns, "Be sober, be vigilant; your adversary the devil walks about like a roaring lion, seeking whom he may devour."

The devil would love to devour us and everyone around us. When we listen to his accusations, we give him an opening to devour. When we speak his accusations against others, we allow him to devour them through us. What a contradiction to the victory Jesus won for all of us!

We must not allow the devil's accusations to come out of our mouths to attack ourselves or others. Today, let us become a voice for salvation and illuminate Jesus Christ's victory in every life we reach.

Prayer

Father, in Jesus' name, I praise You. You are wonderful, and Your works are wonderful. Thank You for sending Jesus to defeat our accuser. I ask You to forgive me for ever siding with him against Your creation or against You. I dedicate to speaking Your words of victory over all people, and words of praise to You, in Jesus' name. Amen.

Out of the Mouth of Babes

The Bible lists many reasons to pray, and one of them is to silence the voice of the enemy. First Peter 5:8-9 says, "Your enemy the devil prowls around like a roaring lion looking for someone to devour. Resist him, standing firm in the faith."

As believers, we have the authority to resist the enemy through prayer in the name of Jesus.

> Out of the mouth of babes and nursing infants You have ordained strength, because of Your enemies, that You may silence the enemy and the avenger.
>
> Psalm 8:2 NKJV

That power is not limited to adult believers. According to God's plan, children have the strength in their mouths to silence the enemy.

In Matthew 21, the prophecy of Psalm 8:2 is fulfilled:

> When the chief priests and the teachers of the law saw the wonderful things he did and the children shouting in the temple area, "Hosanna to the Son of David," they were indignant.
>
> "Do you hear what these children are saying?" they asked him. "Yes," replied Jesus, "have you never read, 'From the lips of children and infants you have ordained praise'?"
>
> Matthew 21:15,16

The enemy will always try to silence praise of the Most High God, but the strength in the mouths of God's children invariably silences the enemy.

As a mother, you have the privilege of instructing your children to use the strength God has given them to stop the enemy's attempts to avert the plan of God. That strength within your children will grow as you empower them with instruction from the Word of God of their rights as believers.

Your example will be the best teaching tool as you instruct your kids in their authority over the enemy. When he tries to enter your home with sickness, depression, or any of his weapons of darkness, resist him in the name of Jesus. You don't have to shout or put on a show; simply stand in your authority—and watch him flee.

> Submit yourselves, then, to God. Resist the devil, and he will flee from you.

> James 4:7

The devil trembles when he sees children of God who know their rights—whether those children are three or ninety-three. By your example and your instruction, lead your children into an understanding of their rights as sons and daughters of God.

Take a Break

Teach your children about their God-given authority.

Your Personal Spring

"Whoever drinks the water I give him will never thirst. Indeed, the water I give him will become in him a spring of water welling up to eternal life."
John 4:13,14

On His way from Judea to Galilee, Jesus passed through a town called Sychar in Samaria. In Sychar, He sat down to rest at Jacob's well. Soon a Samaritan woman came to draw water from the well. Seeing that Jesus was Jewish, she probably bowed her head uncomfortably, drew the water quickly, and expected to quietly depart with the water. However, a parched voice broke through her silence, asking, "Will you give me a drink?" (v. 7).

Having experienced years of segregation from the Jews, this woman was completely taken aback. "You are a Jew and I am a Samaritan woman," she said. *Perhaps He didn't realize,* she might have reasoned. "How can you ask me for a drink?" (v. 7).

Jesus' voice had broken into this woman's God-silent world, and it was about to change her life. "If you knew the gift of God and who it is that asks you for a drink," He said, "you would have asked him and he would have given you living water" (v. 10). He continued:

> "Everyone who drinks this water will be thirsty again, but whoever drinks the water I give him will never thirst. Indeed, the water I give him will become in him a spring of water welling up to eternal life."
>
> John 4:13,14

Jesus offered this woman living water that would quench every thirst. She had been trying to satisfy her thirst for God with human relationships. Jesus said, "You have had five husbands, and the man you now have is not your husband" (v. 17). Suddenly the woman knew He was a prophet, and she said, "I know that Messiah...is coming. When he comes, he will explain everything to us." Jesus said, "I who speak am he" (v. 26).

Jesus identified Himself as the Messiah, and the woman dared to believe. When she returned home, she told all of her friends, and through her testimony many came to Jesus and received the living water that never runs dry. If you have received Jesus, He has become within you a spring of water that wells up every moment of your earthly life and continues to well up to eternal life. Drink deeply of Jesus today. He satisfies!

Prayer

Father, in Jesus' name, I drink deeply of the living water You are in me. Jesus, let Your spring of salvation bubble over in me, touching everyone around me with Your supernatural substance that satisfies, heals, and saves. I praise You, Lord, for being a well of life to me, my family, and my friends. Amen.

The Power of Friendship

Do you remember when you entered the league of mothers—the day you held your child in your arms for the very first time? Suddenly you were a part of a society that perhaps you never realized existed. You discovered a whole new series of experiences and emotions that countless women throughout history under-

> Holy Father, keep them and care for them—all those you have given me—so that they will be united just as we are.
> John 17:11

stood and realized how much you needed the guidance and the friendship of other mothers.

When Mary became pregnant with Jesus by the Holy Spirit, she went immediately to stay with her cousin Elizabeth, who was pregnant with John the Baptist. As soon as Elizabeth heard Mary's voice, her child leaped in her womb. There was a deep connection in the Spirit between these mothers and their children. The Holy Spirit spoke through them, and they rejoiced over the fulfilling of God's eternal plan of redemption in and through them and their children. (Luke 1:39-56.)

God desires to give us friendships like that of Elizabeth and Mary. He wants mothers to be a refuge for one another to turn to in time of need and in time of rejoicing. He wants us to be able to speak freely to one another under the anointing of the Holy Spirit. He wants us to be able to lift up His name and rejoice together over the fulfilling of His plan in each other's lives and the lives of our children.

God wants us to have the support and advice of godly friends. Proverbs 12:26 says, "The godly give good advice to their friends." When God leads us to godly friends, we will need to remember that good advice is not always what we want to hear. It can pull us out of our comfort zones and sometimes stings, but we need to remember that "wounds from a friend can be trusted, but an enemy multiplies kisses" (Prov. 27:6).

Above all, we need to remember that we have a friend whose love will never fail us. John 15:13 says, "Greater love has no one than this, that he lay down his life for his friends." Jesus wants our friendship more than anything—so much that He gave His life to us to attain it. He will be there for us through every situation.

Prayer

Father, I dedicate myself to being a godly friend who willingly gives and receives godly advice, rejoices over the fulfilling of Your will in others' lives, and always supports others in prayer and love. Lord, I pray that You would change lives through me, in Jesus' name. Amen.

Precious in His Sight

Do you recall the day you brought your child home for the first time—the joy and the anxiety of calling this perfect being your own? Deep inside you felt the weight of value God placed on this child, and you wanted to become the best parent you could be in order to give this child more than you ever had.

> "Can a mother forget the baby at her breast and have no compassion on the child she has borne? Though she may forget, I will not forget you!"
>
> Isaiah 49:15

Whether that day in your life was yesterday or ten years ago, God wants you to know that He still holds your child close to His heart. He sent Jesus to demonstrate His love and honor for His children. In Matthew 18:3-6, He acknowledges children's ability to believe in Him and pronounces harsh judgment on any who would deter them from walking with Him.

In Matthew 18:10, He speaks of the continual attentiveness of God and His angels to the well-being of children. His statement is a warning to any who would harm them, yet an encouragement to any who pursue their welfare.

for Moms

Take heed that ye despise not one of these little ones; for I say unto you, That in heaven their angels do always behold the face of my Father which is in heaven.

In Matthew 19:13-15, He welcomes the little children and lays His hands on them:

Then some children were brought to Him so that He might lay His hands on them and pray; and the disciples rebuked them. But Jesus said, "Let the children alone, and do not hinder them from coming to Me; for the kingdom of heaven belongs to such as these. When he had placed his hands on them, he went on from there."

With His welcome, Jesus succinctly conveys God's value for these young ones; and with His blessing, He administers the power of God to them to pursue Him all of their days.

Today, we are privileged to bring our children to Jesus so that they can know Him, believe in Him, and receive His blessing and anointing in their lives. We have the responsibility to live right before them and before the God who is continually watching over them. And we have the mandate to esteem them, for they are precious in His sight.

Take a Break

Remind your kids how precious they are to God—and to you.

Continual Praise

Nearing the end of his reign as king of Israel, David prepared all of the building materials his son Solomon would need for the construction of the Temple. Then he gave assignments to the descendants of Levi for service in the temple. Among them was the mandate to give thanks and praise to the Lord each morning and evening.

> And each morning and evening they stood before the Lord to sing songs of thanks and praise to him.
>
> I Chronicles 23:30 NLT

Today we, too, have an important responsibility. The Bible tells us that by His sacrifice on the cross, Jesus made us kings and priests (Rev. 1:6; 5:10), and our "body is the temple of the Holy Ghost..." (1 Cor. 6:19). As priests in our individual temples, we need to thank and praise God every day.

David's instruction to the Levites was to thank and praise the Lord twice daily—at the beginning and at the end of each day. Taking it even further, Paul wrote that we should "always give thanks for everything to God the Father in the name of our Lord Jesus Christ" (Eph. 5:20

NLT). As believers, we can thank and praise God all day long, every day!

Not only is it important for us to fulfill the personal assignment of continual thanksgiving and praise, but as mothers we have another vital assignment. The Bible says, "A wise woman builds her house..." (Prov. 14:1 NLT). Just as David provided the building materials for the construction of the temple, we can provide for our children the building materials for the construction of their lives upon the foundation of the Word of God. Then, like David, we can assign them the task of daily praise and thanksgiving.

As God-appointed leaders in our homes, our first action in incorporating praise is to practice it ourselves. Remember: King David didn't just tell the Levites to do it; He equipped them with the instruments for the task. (1 Chron. 23:5.) Furthermore, he had lived it himself since his days in the sheep fields.

As mothers, we need to equip our children with instruments to praise God: our example of a life of praise and tools for worshipful expression. If they are musically gifted, we can equip them with musical instruments. If they are artistic, we can give them paints and canvases or pens and paper. If they love nature, we can provide instruments for them to see and study the wonders of God's creation. Most importantly, we can support them as they use their voices to verbally express thanks and praise to God—every day.

Take a Break

Along with each of your children, list at least three reasons you are thankful to God today.

Sex Education

> For this reason a man will leave his father and mother and be united to his wife, and they will become one flesh.
>
> Genesis 2:24

God made man and woman sexual creatures. He gave each of us the anatomy to reproduce, as well as the capacity to enjoy sexual pleasure. Sex is a beautiful gift from God and He wants us to enjoy it. Because it is so important, when do we teach our kids about sex, and how much do we say?

The fact is that we live in a society that bombards our kids with sexual images every day. Whether we choose to teach them about sex or not, they will learn. The question is, what do we want them to learn, and what does God want them to learn?

From birth our children can be given a healthy, scriptural look at the beautiful gift of sexuality. The first thing we can teach them is that God created them, male and female, and each is a wonderful creation. As they continue to grow, they will need to learn God's parameters for sex, which are first mentioned in Genesis 2:24.

A man is to be united to his wife and to become one flesh with her. Notice: marriage comes first, uniting comes second, and finally the two become one flesh. The phrase "one flesh" indicates not only the sexual unity between the two but also the unbreakable bond between their persons resulting from the sex act. In God's eyes, they become one. In the parameters of marriage, this is a beautiful image; but outside of it, it becomes the image of bondage and imprisonment.

While today's public sex education proliferates the idea that pregnancy and sexually transmitted diseases are the worst possible consequences of premarital sex, the truth is that the act itself can injure lives. Sex can attach people who would not otherwise have become attached; and when they separate, they lose a piece of themselves forever.

Without a full-life commitment, sex can destroy not only a couple but their two individual lives. Some may argue that a full-life commitment can happen without a marriage. However, the covenant of marriage is a clear indication to both a man and a woman that each is committed to the other for life. Without it, one or the other must deal with the fear that the union between them— and, therefore, they themselves—will be broken.

While the consequences of premarital sex are dismal, the rewards of sex in marriage are beautiful. Children need to know that sex is a wonderful, God-given experience to be shared between a man and a woman who have committed their entire lives (not just their bodies) to one another. They need to know that sex is only worthwhile when it is shared between a man and a woman who want to remain united for life and have demonstrated that desire in the covenant of marriage—and then it is a precious gift to both.

Prayer

Father, I pray that You'll help me to speak honestly with my children about Your gift of sexuality. Help me not to shy away from teaching them the truth. I pray that You would open up the lines of communication between my kids and me so that I can share Your truth with them and encourage them to wait for Your best for them—a loving marriage relationship. Lord, give my kids the courage and the wisdom to protect their virginity until they are united in marriage, and then reward them with a joyful relationship, in Jesus' name. Amen.

Reclaim Your Emotions

Have you ever felt as if your emotions were completely out of your control? Perhaps something aggravated you, and your feelings just took over. Your heart raced, your face flushed, your fists clenched, and you blurted whatever ugly emotion

> For all who are led by the Spirit of God are children of God.
> Romans 8:14 NLT

you were feeling. At one time or another—or perhaps on a fairly regular basis—each of us has allowed emotions to take control.

God gave us emotions, and they are essentially good. Some of them help us enjoy our daily experiences, and some of them help us avoid danger. Emotions often serve us well. However, when emotions take control of our actions, they can cause major problems for us and for the people around us.

The apostle Paul tells us in the book of Galatians that if we live in the spirit, we will not gratify the lusts of the flesh. (Gal. 5:16.) Our flesh desires to control us through our emotions, but that is not always beneficial to us or to the people around us. It might feel good to let anger loose with a pound of the fist or a verbal assault, or to let self-pity express itself with tears and complaints; however, acting on those negative feelings often hurts us and others.

We have felt the ongoing tremor of bitterness even after we've cried and complained in self-pity. We have felt the floods of guilt when we've acted out in anger. We have discovered for ourselves how destructive our emotions can be when they take control. We need to know how to reclaim self-control.

For the difficult task of controlling our emotions, God gave us His Spirit to take back the reigns and restore peace to our souls. Any negative emotion listed in Galatians 5:19-21 can be overcome by leaning on the power of the Holy Spirit. When we "keep in step with the Spirit" (Gal. 5:25), we overcome the impulses of destructive emotions.

When we feel weak, and our emotions feel strong, we can lean on God's grace that is sufficient for us (2 Cor. 12:9) and walk in the fruit of the Spirit instead. (Gal. 5:22,23.) In our weakness, God's power will enable us to reclaim control over our emotions and produce the good fruit of His Spirit.

Take a Break

Submit your emotions to the power of God's Spirit and His Word.

Good Friends for Your Kids

Children need friends. In truth, we all do. Friends pick us up when we fall, and they rejoice when we rise. Good friends play, laugh, cry, and pray together, and they provide each other with a tangible image of Jesus' love:

> I am a friend to all who fear you, to all who follow your precepts.
>
> Psalm 119:63

> Greater love has no one than this, that he lay down his life for his friends.... I have called you friends....
>
> John 15:13,15

While the company of friends brightens our lives, "bad company corrupts good character" (1 Cor. 15:33). The character of our friends makes a vital impact on our character. As mothers we may train our children in God's ways, but the friends they choose will deeply affect their long-term commitment to that training.

For this reason, part of the training we give our children must address the importance of choosing good friends. Throughout our children's time at home, we can help them with the task of making good relationship choices. We should be well acquainted with our children's friends, as well as their friends' families. We should be observant of our children's behavior both when they are with their friends and afterward. Most importantly, we should lean on the wisdom of the Holy Spirit. If our hearts tell us something is wrong with a relationship in our child's life, whether we have a logical reason or not, we need to heed the Holy Spirit's voice. He knows so much better than we do, and His wisdom will keep our children safe from every kind of harm.

The Bible is packed with examples of good friendships that we can introduce to our children when they are very young and remind them of often as they grow. Our children will be encouraged to see the results of bonding with people of good character as seen in the lives of such biblical characters as David and Jonathan (1 Sam. 18-23; 2 Sam. 1-21); Daniel, Shadrach, Meshach, and Abednego (Dan. 3); Mary and Elizabeth (Luke 1); Jesus, Mary, Martha, and Lazarus (Luke 10:38-42; 16); and the first members of the New Testament church (Acts 1).

As we teach our children about choosing friends, we need to remind them especially of the example of Jesus, who reached the lost through friendliness (Mark 2:17; Luke 7:34) and offered His friendship to those who followed God's commands (John 15:14). Our kids' closest friends should be those who follow God's commands. When they are with acquaintances who do not, they need to remember to be leaders and not followers—and we should be diligent to help them make the distinction.

The most important thing we can do to help our children make the right choices in friendship is to ensure their friendship with Jesus.

> God...invited you into this wonderful friendship with his Son, Jesus Christ our Lord.

> 1 Corinthians 1:9

When our kids know Him personally, and when they seek Him for themselves, they will make good choices in all of their human relationships—and their closest Friend will be glorified because of it.

Prayer

Father, I ask You to send good friends to each of my children. Holy Spirit, guide me and each of my kids in our spirits as my children build friendships. Help my children to discern between good and bad company, and help them influence others with Your Word and Your love, in Jesus' name. Amen.

A Mother's Spiritual Care

And my God shall supply all your need according to His riches in glory by Christ Jesus.
Philippians
4:19 NKJV

The ability to care for our children's physical needs comes instinctively to us. As new mothers we learn how to feed, clothe, bathe, shelter, and provide a restful environment for our babies. However, along with these physical needs, our children have spiritual needs—and God has supplied them all.

For example, we bathe our children regularly with water, soap, and wash cloths. Likewise, we need to bathe them spiritually every day. Ephesians 5:25-27 tells us that Jesus washes us with the water of His Word. Therefore, we need to introduce our children to Jesus and His Word, which will cleanse their hearts and keep them spiritually pure.

We also need to feed our children spiritual food every day just like we feed them natural food daily. Jesus said, "I am the bread of life. He who comes to me will never go hungry, and he who believes in me will never be thirsty" (John 6:35). We need to see that our children are spiritually nourished with the words and the power of Jesus, who satisfies every need.

As we provide physical shelter to keep our children safe from the elements and dangers outside, we must also teach our children that God is their shelter and protector. Beginning when they are in the womb, we can speak to them of the eternal security in their Father's loving arms.

It is important to encourage our children to rest their bodies and their spirits. Psalm 46:10 says, "Be still, and know that I am God." We need to teach our children that true spiritual rest occurs regardless of the surrounding circumstances—that it comes from being still and knowing God is in control and will always keep them safe and victorious.

God knows our children's needs, and He wants to become their sole source of supply. As you lead your children to Him, pray and trust that they will learn to lean increasingly on Him to meet all of their needs—physical, emotional, and spiritual.

In order to properly care for the spirits of the children God has placed in your care, you will need to replenish your own. Remember the One who has promised to meet all of your needs, and run to Him daily. His supply is more than enough!

Prayer

Father, I commit to replenish my spirit in the Word and in You every day. I want to properly nurture my children's spirits. Help me to give them all they need by giving them You. In Jesus' name I pray. Amen.

Rejoice Over Your Children

In the Bible, we find God repeatedly approving of His children. Perhaps the most memorable account of God's verbal approval occurs at His Son's baptism. Matthew 3:17 says, "And a voice from heaven said, 'This is my Son, whom I love; with him I am well pleased.'" At that moment, God publicly honored His Son.

> The Lord your God...will take great delight in you, he will quiet you with his love, he will rejoice over you with singing.
> Zephaniah 3:17

As mothers, we have the precious opportunity to speak approval into the lives of our children—to praise them, just as God praises us. (Zeph. 3:17.) Admittedly, at times it seems there is little in our children to praise, but must it be any different for our heavenly Father with us? Not one of is without sin (Rom. 3:23), yet God rejoices over us.

Zephaniah 3:15 says, "The Lord has taken away your punishment, he has turned back your enemy." Eternal redemption has come to all of us through Jesus' sacrifice on the cross, and when we receive it we are no longer subject to the punishment our former sins deserved. We are not spiritual slaves or orphans. Rather, we are children of God.

> For [the Spirit which] you have now received [is] not a spirit of slavery to put you once more in bondage to fear, but you have received the Spirit of adoption [the Spirit producing sonship] in [the bliss of] which we cry, Abba (Father)! Father!

Romans 8:15 AMP

As our Father, God gives us assignments and has high expectations of us. He knows that through Christ, we can do all things (Phil. 4:13), and He always sends us out on assignment with a word of approval. For example, when He sent Gideon into battle against all odds, He said, "The Lord is with you, mighty warrior" (Judges 6:12). When He called Saul, He explained, "This man is my chosen instrument to carry my name before the Gentiles and their kings and before the people of Israel" (Acts 9:15).

In each case, God named the person what He needed him to be so he could fulfill His plan. He pronounced Gideon a "mighty warrior," and Saul His "chosen instrument." In context, we know that neither man appeared to be what God was calling him. Gideon was self-described as the least in the weakest clan (Judges 6:15), and Saul had recently been "breathing out murderous threats against the Lord's disciples" (Acts 9:1). Yet both men became exactly what God had called them.

In the same way, we can speak words of encouragement, approval, and faith over our children so that they can fulfill their God-given assignments. We can speak positive words over their spiritual condition, their behavior, their academic efforts, and everything about them.

As we speak words of faith over our children in their hearing, we fill them with the confidence and faith to become what we have said. Today, let's have faith in our children. Let's speak words of encouragement over them. Let's spend time rejoicing over them—just as their heavenly Father does. Then let's watch them rise in His strength to meet His expectation and fulfill His calling.

Take a Break

Speak acceptance, approval, and faith-filled words over each of your children today.

Release the Burdens

For You shall break the yoke of their burden and the staff on their shoulders, the rod of their oppressor.

Isaiah 9:4 NASB

If your life feels heavy today, God wants to help you get rid of the burden. Isaiah 9:6 describes how the yoke of burden would be broken: "For a child will be born to us, a son will be given to us; and the government will rest on His shoulders."

Born in Bethlehem, Jesus fulfilled this prophecy and broke the yoke of burden that rested on our shoulders. A yoke is "a curved piece of wood... fitted on the neck of oxen for the purpose of binding to them the traces by which they might draw the plough."[2] Since the fall of man, the devil bound an invisible yoke around every human neck so that we could haul every kind of spiritual, mental, and physical destruction. When Jesus sacrificed His life and became sin for us, He removed that yoke.

When we become Christians, we are freed from the devil's yoke and receive the Lord's.

"Come to me, all you who are weary and burdened, and I will give you rest. Take my yoke upon you and learn from me, for I am gentle and humble in heart, and you will find rest for your souls. For my yoke is easy and my burden is light."

Matthew 11:28-30

We exchange the painful yoke and heavy burden of sin for Jesus' yoke, which is the light burden of His Word. His Word is a yoke and burden if we try to perform it in our own strength, but Jesus wants us to perform God's will in His strength. He wants us to be free. Galatians 5:1 says, "It is for freedom that Christ has set us free. Stand firm, then, and do not let yourselves be burdened again by a yoke of slavery."

No runner wins a race when she's looking at the starting line. She must look to the finish. We look to the finish by keeping our eyes on Jesus. (v. 4.) If we want to win this race to which God has called us, we must let go of the burden of the past, accept Jesus' offer to shoulder the weight of the yoke and burden of His call, and keep looking to Him. We began this journey of faith in Him, and we will finish it in His strength.

Take a Break

Drop the burden of the past, take on Jesus' easy yoke and light burden, and accomplish His will in His strength.

A Lifetime of Honor

> But if a widow has children or grandchildren, these should learn first of all to put their religion into practice by caring for their own family and so repaying their parents and grandparents, for this is pleasing to God.
>
> I Timothy 5:4

During the formation of the New Testament church, the believers were given specific instructions for caring for the people in need among them. In a letter to Timothy, the apostle Paul thoroughly outlined the church's responsibility for widows. The young widows were instructed to remarry and care for their families, and the elderly ones (over 60 years) were entrusted to their children's and grandchildren's care. The remaining elderly widows were supported by the church, and those who met certain qualifications became part of the ministerial team of the church and were compensated as such. (1 Tim. 5:9,10,17.)[3] The elder men of the church were also compensated for their work in the church. (1 Tim. 5:17.)

Today, many people lean on the government to support the elderly among them. However, as God's children, we are called to honor our fathers and mothers. This honor doesn't end when we move out of our parents' homes. It continues throughout our entire lives.

One day Jesus rebuked the Pharisees and teachers of the law for misleading their followers in this regard. He said:

> "God said, 'Honor your father and mother' and 'Anyone who curses his father or mother must be put to death.' But you say that if a man says to his father or mother, 'Whatever help you might otherwise have received from me is a gift devoted to God,' he is not to 'honor his father' with it."

Matthew 15:4-6

With these words, Jesus revealed to us that a sign of honoring our parents is our supporting them throughout our adulthood. He also revealed that when we fail to help them when it is in our power to do so, we are cursing them.

The word *honor* in this verse means "to estimate, fix the value; to revere, venerate."[4] How we care for our parents demonstrates how much we value them and their God-given position in our lives. Whether we've had good or bad experiences with them, we must honor them not according to those experiences or our feelings, but according to the Word of God.

When our parents become dependent on others for care, we must be the first at their sides to offer our support. We need to find out what our parents need from us and do all in our power to help them. When we honor our parents in this way, God will honor us and help us meet the task. If we ask Him to, He will give us the wisdom, the courage, and the resources to follow His Word by honoring our parents as He wants us to all of our days.

Take a Break

With your husband, pray for your parents and his. Find a way to honor them today.

Training Future Husbands and Wives

As moms, we have a lot to think about every day, but how often do we look ahead through the years to the time when our sons will be husbands and our daughters will be wives? The way we rear our kids greatly influences the way they will one day treat their spouses. Our kids notice every day how we treat our

> For this reason a man will leave his father and mother and be united to his wife, and they will become one flesh.
>
> Genesis 2:24

husbands and how we allow them to treat us and each other. They watch, they listen, and they learn.

Our homes are where our children learn the skills to resolve conflict. Proverbs 17:17 NKJV says, "A brother is born for adversity," and we use sibling rivalry to help our children peacefully settle their disputes and learn the skill of conflict resolution.

As we teach our children necessary life skills, we must remain conscious of our example. We need to consistently take responsibility for our actions and do all that we can to maintain peace in each of our relationships. Hebrews 12:18 NKJV says, "If it is possible, as much as depends on you, live peaceably with all men."

To maintain peace with our family members, we have to overcome one immense impediment—the reluctance to say "I'm sorry." We must be more interested in doing what's right than in being right in our own minds. If we make a mistake or hurt someone, we need to acknowledge what we've done—whether or not we have been wronged. Rather than ruminating over our injuries, we need to ask God and our loved one to forgive us for the pain we have inflicted and seek restoration—as quickly as possible.

Ephesians 4:26 instructs us, "Do not let the sun go down while you are still angry." When we wait to resolve conflict, we allow ourselves, our loved one, and our relationship to remain broken. Resolution restores wholeness. The sooner it occurs, the better.

Today, let's use our example and our influence wisely as our children grow into men and women. Let's keep in mind our future sons- and daughters-in-law and train our children to be a blessing to them.

Prayer

Father, I pray for my children's future spouses. Lord, I want to bless them by training my children to love them, respect them, and live peacefully with them. Help me give them a good example to look to as they build their own lives and marriages, in Jesus' name. Amen.

God's Word on Health

Seeing our child suffer is the deepest pain we can endure. In I Kings 17:17-24, we read about a mother who felt the worst possible pain—her son's death. She bitterly asks the prophet Elijah, "What do you have against me, man of God? Did you come to remind me of my sin and kill my son?"

> Dear friend, I am praying that all is well with you and that your body is as healthy as I know your soul is.
>
> 3 John 2 NLT

Elijah's response and the subsequent events reveal the heart of God not only for this woman and her child, but also for us and our children. On behalf of this heartbroken woman, Elijah cried to the Lord for God's healing power to revive her son. The Lord heard Elijah's cry and raised the boy from the dead.

Malachi speaks of the One whom God would send who, like Elijah, would bear us up in His arms and intercede for our healing:

> But for you who revere my name, the sun of righteousness will rise with healing in its wings.
>
> Malachi 4:2

Isaiah also prophesies of God making healing available to us:

> But he was pierced for our transgressions, he was crushed for our iniquities; the punishment that brought us peace was upon him, and by his wounds we are healed.

Isaiah 53:5

Who is the sun of righteousness with healing in His wings? Who is the One who was pierced and crushed, whose wounds have purchased our healing? First Timothy 2:5 identifies Him: "For there is one God and one mediator between God and men, the man Christ Jesus." Jesus is the One who, like Elijah, bears us up in His arms to the place of healing—His Father's presence.

In order to attain the healing Jesus offers, we need two things: His Word and faith. Psalm 107:20 speaks of the former: "He sent forth his word and healed them; he rescued them from the grave." Luke 8:48 speaks of the latter: "Then [Jesus] said to her, 'Daughter, your faith has healed you. Go in peace'" (Luke 8:48).

Jesus has brought us healing, and the way we receive it is by receiving Him through His Word—because He and His Word are one. (See John 1:1-18.) We receive Him with our faith, which comes by hearing the Word of God. (Rom. 8:17.) The most important thing we can do to attain divine healing is to spend time reading, meditating on, speaking, and listening to His Word.

If your children need healing, focus on Scriptures that refer to God's healing nature. In the Old Testament, God told His people, "I am the Lord, who heals you" (Ex. 15:26). Psalm 103:3 says that He "forgives all your sins and heals all your diseases." God is a healer, and He wants you and your kids to be healthy every day of your lives. Mark 6:56 says, "...all who touched [Jesus] were healed." And 3 John 2 says, "Dear friend, I pray that you may enjoy good health and that all may go well with you, even as your soul is getting along well."

You can never overdose on the Word of God, and it works as a preventive medicine as well as a cure. Teach your children to take a regular dose of healing by daily reading and speaking God's Word. Then, if sickness tries to touch anyone in your house, treat it on the spot with the Word of God. God's Word is powerful because it contains His unconquerable will—and His will is your health. Receive and believe His Word, and expect God's healing for your family today.

Prayer

Father, in Jesus' name, I receive Your healing today. I commit to study and to instruct my family in Your Word so Your promises become our daily experience. We receive Your healing touch in our lives today and every day, in Jesus' name. Amen.

Your Spiritual Thermostat

For the kingdom of God is not a matter of eating and drinking, but of righteousness, peace and joy in the Holy Spirit.

Romans 14:17

Just as we set the thermostat to determine the temperature of our homes, we can set our spiritual thermostats to determine the spiritual atmosphere of our homes. When we are full of peace, our families reflect that peace. When we are full of stress, our families reflect that stress. Our attitude sets the spiritual tone in our homes.

Romans 14:17 tells us that heaven is "righteousness, peace and joy in the Holy Spirit" (Rom. 14:17). When we stay close to heaven by staying close to Jesus, we bring heaven's atmosphere into our homes. When we spend time with Him, we draw our family into His presence and our families experience heaven on earth.

When we live in God's presence, His Word determines our actions and our behavior. We experience heaven's righteousness when Jesus reigns in us, and His peace becomes our peace. Jesus said, "Peace I leave with you; my peace I give you. I do not give to you as the world gives. Do not let your hearts be troubled and do not be afraid" (John 14:27).

The peace of the world and the peace of Jesus are quite different from one another. While the peace of the world is dependent on circumstances, the peace of Jesus prevails independent of the circumstances. When our families seek God, His peace causes us to remain stable and whole no matter what troubles face us.

When we live in God's presence, we live in His joy. God's joy is impervious to attack. When difficulties arise, God's Word says, "Don't be dejected and sad, for the joy of the Lord is your strength!" (Neh. 8:10). God's joy keeps our families laughing together no matter what happens and attracts our neighbors and friends to Him.

> But thanks be to God, who always leads us in triumphal procession in Christ and through us spreads everywhere the fragrance of the knowledge of him
>
> 2 Corinthians 2:14

By welcoming the presence of God into our lives, we welcome the presence of heaven into our homes. We welcome the heavenly atmosphere of righteousness, peace, and joy in the Holy Spirit. When we remain in God, our families find wholeness and the lost find Him through the fragrance of heaven on us and in our homes.

Take a Break

Let righteousness, peace, and joy rule in your home today by spending time in God's presence.

Nurturing Your Child's Gift

Even before your children were conceived, God had a specific purpose for each one. He knew where and when and to whom they would be born. He knew you would be their mom, and He knew how your training would impact their pursuit of His call.

> Your eyes saw my unformed body. All the days ordained for me were written in your book before one of them came to be.
>
> Psalm 139:16

As a mom, you play a vital role in confirming the purpose of God in each of your children, which He established long before you knew them.

> "I knew you before I formed you in your mother's womb. Before you were born I set you apart and appointed you as my spokesman to the world."
>
> Jeremiah 1:5 NLT

Your children need to know that they have a unique, God-given purpose—that they were not arbitrarily placed here on earth. They need to know that they are valuable—and their greatest sense of value will come when they know God's value for them, demonstrated in His sacrifice for each one:

> For God so loved the world that he gave his only
> Son, so that everyone who believes in him will not
> perish but have eternal life.
>
> John 3:16 NLT

As your children grow, they will exhibit unique strengths, abilities, and talents. These are gifts from God for their use as they pursue His calling. As a mom, you can help your children discover and develop these unique gifts.

To do this, you will need to spend quality time with your children. As you and your children interact, or simply as all of you go about your day, consciously observe your children's interests and favorite activities. Be aware of their achievements, and be consistent in applauding their efforts.

Most people are sensitive to applause or criticism of their gifts. Keep this in mind as you interact with your children. Your attention and praise will prompt them to continue to use their gifts, but your criticism or disinterest may halt their growth in the area of their giftedness.

In the church God has given us many gifts, and each one has a purpose. It is not to lie dormant but to be used:

> Each one should use whatever gift he has received
> to serve others, faithfully administering God's grace in
> its various forms.
>
> 1 Peter 4:10

The gift God has given each of us is a demonstration of His grace to be given to others. Encourage your children's efforts to use their gifts to bless others. If your child has the gift of showing mercy, for example, support her as she shows mercy to family members, neighbors, friends, and ministries. If your child is musically talented, encourage him as he uses his gift to worship God and to minister to others. If your child is multitalented, encourage her to focus on one gift at a time to use to bless others; in time, she will be able to bless others with all of the gifts God has given her.

Sometimes we don't realize the gifts that are within ourselves, let alone within our children. Sometimes it takes more than our physical senses to discern these precious qualities God has placed inside. For this reason, we need to depend on the Holy Spirit as we nurture our children's gifts. He knows God's purpose for each one, and He will enlighten us to see the gifts He has given them to use for His glory.

Prayer

Father, in Jesus' name, show me the gifts You have placed in my children. Help me to encourage their gifts and their desire to demonstrate Your grace to others by using those gifts. Lord, in Jesus' name, I pray in faith that with their gifts, my children will fulfill Your purpose for Your glory and draw many to You. Amen.

Make Disciples

> Therefore go and make disciples of all nations, baptizing them in the name of the Father and of the Son and of the Holy Spirit, and teaching them to obey everything I have commanded you.
>
> Matthew 28:19,20

Before His ascension into heaven, Jesus gave His disciples the Great Commission to make disciples of all nations. His disciples began immediately to spread the word of the glorious gospel of Christ, impacting nations of people. As time passed, the gospel story continued to be told until it reached you. Over the past 2000-plus years people have taken to heart Jesus' Great Commission and have made for Him disciples of their acquaintances, friends, parents, siblings, and children.

What has empowered believers to carry out the assignment? In Acts 1:8, Jesus tells His disciples, "But you will receive power when the Holy Spirit comes on you; and you will be my witnesses in Jerusalem, and in all Judea and Samaria, and to the ends of the earth." The Holy Spirit empowers you to make disciples of your children.

The family is a great influence, and God has long used this structure to perpetuate His covenant with His

people. For example, in Deuteronomy 11, He speaks
directly to parents:

> Fix these words of mine in your hearts and
> minds.... Teach them to your children, talking about
> them when you sit at home and when you walk along
> the road, when you lie down and when you get up.
> Write them on the doorframes of your houses and on
> your gates.
>
> Deuteronomy 11:18-20

With our words and actions, at every opportunity
every day, we are to teach our children the words of God.
When we're in the car with them, when we're eating
dinner together, we are to speak and live out the words of
God. We are to make our children disciples of Christ, as
we are disciples of Christ.

In Isaiah 54:13, God promises His people, "All your
children shall be taught by the Lord, and great shall be the
peace of your children." Claim this verse for your family. It
is God's promise, so keep your spiritual ears tuned to His
instruction, be ever ready to deliver His instruction to
your children, and expect that God Himself will instruct
them. Then great will be the peace of your children
because they will be disciples of the Prince of Peace.

Take a Break

Choose a portion of Scripture to study, and look for opportunities to teach your children what you have learned.

When Kids Rebel

When kids rebel it's tempting to place the blame on someone, and too often mothers blame themselves. The truth is that kids have wills, and they sometimes use them to do the wrong thing—just as all of us have done:

> All have sinned and fall short of the glory of God.
>
> Romans 3:23

"But while he was still a long way off, his father saw him and was filled with compassion for him; he ran to his son, threw his arms around him and kissed him."

Luke 15:20

For the first years of our children's lives, we can and should supervise their behavior and attitudes closely. When they rebel against authority, we should lovingly correct them and steer them back onto God's path—which begins with their obedience to us. However, even when children have walked the right path for years, they sometimes stray.

Our longing for our children's well-being is the same longing that our Father feels for each of us. His heart ached when Adam and Eve turned against Him in rebellion, and His heart still aches when any one of us is far from Him. The will God gave each of us gives us the freedom to refuse Him, but we can only imagine the immense joy He feels when we use that will to choose Him!

If your child has chosen to refuse God, you can trust that His Word will light his way back home. (Ps. 119:105.) If your child has wandered from you in rebellion, God wants you to know you are not alone. He has said, "Never will I leave you; never will I forsake you" (Heb. 13:5). He is right by your side, and He won't ever let you or your child go. His eyes are on you and on everything that concerns you—including your child.

If you feel all hope for your child is gone, He gives you this promise: "'There is hope for your future,' says the Lord. 'Your children will come again to their own land'" (Jer. 31:16 NLT). Hold on to God's powerful promise, and speak it over your child every day.

If your heart aches for your child but you don't know what to do, God gives you His Spirit: "Meanwhile, the moment we get tired in the waiting, God's Spirit is right alongside helping us along. If we don't know how or what to pray, it doesn't matter. He does our praying in and for us, making prayer out of our wordless sighs, our aching groans" (Rom. 8:26 MESSAGE). Ask the Holy Spirit to help you pray, and He will help you pray God's will for your child.

The same Intercessor who will lead you in prayer will remind your children of the truth of God's Word. Jesus promised He would:

> But the Comforter (Counselor, Helper, Intercessor, Advocate, Strengthener, Standby), the Holy Spirit...will teach you all things. And He will cause you to recall (will remind you of, bring to your remembrance) everything I have told you.

John 14:26 AMP

Your children may need a reminder in their hearts of the love and forgiveness that awaits them in God's presence and at home. Even if you can't remind them, the Holy Spirit will—when you pray.

If distance or silence separates you from your child, don't give up on God's ability to bring him back. Entrust your prodigal child to His keeping, and get ready for a joyful reunion—because one day you will see him on the horizon making his way back home.

Take a Break

Speak to each of your children about God's love and forgiveness, and reassure them of your unconditional love.

One Body

> In Christ we who are many form one body, and each member belongs to all the others.
>
> Romans 12:5

The word "church" is used to describe both a local body of believers and the corporate body of Christ—believers worldwide for all time. On an eternal scale, it is most important to be a part of the corporate church—and that happens when we receive salvation. However, without the local church we cannot fully experience, understand, benefit from, or bless the corporate church—the body of Christ.

The local church is an expression of the body of Christ. It is where members of the body spend time together, edify one another, pray with one another, and worship together. Fellowship with other believers increases our anointing individually and corporately. Then we can go out to be witnesses of Jesus and bring more members into the church.

Our children observe not only our choices but our attitudes. They will if we go to church because we feel we have to or if we go because we want to. David said, "It made me glad to hear them say, 'Let's go to the house of the Lord!'" (Ps. 122:1). It will make your children glad to see a smile on your face when you say, "Let's go to church!" Your smile means time in God's presence, being built up in His Word, and joining with the rest of His body to worship Him.

It is no coincidence that the Holy Spirit came to rest on individuals when they were together worshiping Him on the day of Pentecost. After Jesus' resurrection, He told His followers, "Do not leave Jerusalem, but wait for the gift my Father promised, which you have heard me speak about. For John baptized with water, but in a few days you will be baptized with the Holy Spirit" (Acts 1:4). As the believers unified in obedience, reverence, faith, and trust, they received the promise. As a result, they became witnesses to Jerusalem and to the ends of the earth.

Imagine what God can do in and through His body when we continue to unify, joining in one place at one time to honor the one God. This week, make your choice. And remember: Your children are watching.

Prayer

Father, in Jesus' name, I thank You for making me a member of the body of Christ. Help me and my family to unite with other members of the body to worship You and to fulfill Your work. Show us our place in the body so that we can serve You well by serving others. Amen.

God's Ideals

> But he said to me, "My grace is sufficient for you, for my power is made perfect in weakness." Therefore I will boast all the more gladly about my weaknesses, so that Christ's power may rest on me.
>
> 2 Corinthians 12:9

Whatever ideals we have in life, we hold one close to our hearts: We each want to be the perfect mom for our kids. Though every mom's definition of *the perfect mom* is slightly different from the next, every mom has one thing in common: imperfection. The problem is that we're all human, and that means we all fall short of ideal. (Rom. 3:23.)

Ask any mom in the world if she's ever had a moment when she didn't like being a mom, and if she's honest she'll say yes. It's not that she's ever stopped loving her kids, but she has had moments—or even days—when she didn't like the job of motherhood. Those are the days when she feels less than ideal.

The truth is that God isn't into human idealism. He thinks, sees, and feels on a completely different level than we do. He says to each of us,

For as the heavens are higher than the earth, so are my ways higher than your ways, and my thoughts than your thoughts.

Isaiah 55:9

God wants us to let go of our human ideals and standards and cling to Him. He wants us to focus on His strength and His ability to follow His commands—not our own weakness and inability to accomplish our own.

When we demand more of ourselves than God does, we limit our progress in Him. As moms, that means we limit our progress in relationship to our children. God wants each of us to become so dependent on the leading of His Word and His Spirit that we set aside our own agendas and our own ideals and follow solely after His. He wants us to rise above our perspective so that we achieve His.

Until we see our lives as He does, we won't realize the differences between our ideals and His. For example, what we see as a failure, God may see as a victory. We may see a messy kitchen as a failure, but God may see the victory we won by spending extra time attending to our children's needs. We may see an angry outburst as a failure, but God may see the progress we made by responding to a wrongdoing with justice.

for Moms

Until we gain God's perspective on our lives, we may be chasing after an ideal, pressing ourselves to a mark that God never intended us to reach. If we run after our ideals rather than His, we will miss His mark—the only one that matters. But if we press toward His, we will reach it—but not by our own efforts. What we need now, and what we will always need, is God's grace—and in our weakness, He has offered us a sufficient supply. (2 Cor. 12:9.) When we depend on the leading of His Word and His Spirit, and when we settle into the gift of His grace, we become who God wants us to be. May this become our ideal.

Take a Break

Seek God to discover His agenda for your day, and follow it in His strength.

Children, Honor Your Parents

The greatest reward we have as mothers is to know that our children honor God everywhere they go and for the rest of their lives after they leave our homes. For this to happen, we teach them how to honor God in everything they say and do.

God has a plan and destiny for each of our children. He desires to use their gifts to minister to others, and He wants to bless them. He also says that in order for them to fulfill their calling and be blessed, they must honor their parents.

Though our children are ultimately accountable for honoring us, we can help them make the right choice. To do that, we need to honor the position God has placed us in as mothers. Only then will our children understand and respect authority. First Timothy 3:4 says, "He must manage his own family well and see that his children obey him with proper respect." If we don't require our children to obey and respect us, we give them room to disobey and disrespect God and every human's authority.

> Honor your father and your mother, as the Lord your God has commanded you, so that you may live long and that it may go well with you in the land the Lord your God is giving you.
> Deuteronomy 5:16

for Moms

Our children's first step toward learning to honor God is honoring us. Responsibility and honor begin at home under parental instruction. We must be sure that we base our authority on the Word of God. We must lead as He leads. We must honor our word—doing what we say we will do. We must show grace, caring more about each child's well-being than our own agenda. We must reward diligence. We must be motivated by love. In short, we must learn who our Father is and reflect Him to our children.

When we teach our children to honor us and to honor God, we give them the precious opportunity to avoid all of the pain and frustration that rebellion and dis-respect ultimately bring, and we lead them to the land the Lord their God is giving them. That is what true love can do, and that is what we do when we honor God's Word by teaching our children to honor Him.

Prayer

Father, I want my children to honor You all of their days. Help me to realize my responsibility in teaching them to honor You. Help me to base my expectations of them on Your Word and to be led by Your Holy Spirit as I train them in Your way. Thank You for the plans You have for each one of them— plans to prosper them in the places to which You've called them. Use me to help them choose Your path, Lord. In Jesus' name I pray. Amen.

Mothering Your Adult Children

God desires that our children learn through our training how to meet the responsibilities that will face them as adults. Once they get there, He desires that we let them meet the challenges of adulthood in His strength. After years of training,

> Train up a child in the way he should go, and when he is old he will not depart from it.
> Proverbs 22:6 NKJV

they may be more ready for the transition than we are!

For example, when our adult children are faced with important decisions, we may wish we could decide for them. However, we need to consider what God's Word says: "Train up a child in the way he should go, and when he is old he will not depart from it" (Prov. 22:6 NKJV). If we have trained them in the way they should go, we can trust that they will discern God's will for their own lives.

If we haven't trained them in God's ways, their adulthood is not the time for us to start. We need to ask God to father them, Jesus to befriend them, and the Holy Spirit to lead them—and we need to be prepared to offer godly instruction when our children ask. In the meantime, our best ministry tools for reaching them will be our prayers and our godly and loving example.

Even if we think our well-trained children are making unwise decisions, we need to be careful how we respond. If their hearts are open to God's voice, they will know His will for their lives—even more than we will. At this point in their lives, we can help them most by praying for them, encouraging them, and reinforcing our belief in them.

No matter how mature our children become, they will always benefit from knowing we believe in them. Their desire to delight us doesn't stop in preschool, when they beam at their colored pictures on the refrigerator door. That desire for our approval lasts for a lifetime. Knowing their parents are proud of them will give our adult children the assurance they need to confidently reach for their God-given dreams.

If we ourselves haven't received this kind of affirmation from our parents, it may feel uncomfortable to give it to our kids. However, if we want our children to live satisfied and fulfilled lives, we will make the extra effort to demonstrate our love, belief, and delight in them. Remember: Before Jesus entered His earthly ministry, His Father affirmed Him, saying, "You are My beloved Son, in whom I am well pleased" (Mark 1:11).

We should never stop telling our children how pleased we are with them, how beloved they are in our eyes, and how much joy it gives us to call them our own.

When we love them like this, we give them the courage to be the men and women God created them to be—and we give ourselves the gift of a fulfilling and lasting relationship with each one of them.

Take a Break

With a note or a phone call, tell each of your kids, "I love you, I believe in you, and I am proud of you."

Instructions for Marriage

For the husband is the head of the wife as Christ is the head of the church, his body, of which he is the Savior. Now as the church submits to Christ, so also wives should submit to their husbands in everything. Husbands, love your wives, just as Christ loved the church.... Each one of you also must love his wife as he loves himself, and the wife must respect her husband.

Ephesians 5:23-26,33

Through the Bible God gives instructions for marriage that will create joyful and lifelong unions if we follow them. He tells us that the husband (the head of the home) is to love his wife as Christ (the head of the church) loves the church. He is also to love her as he loves himself. The wife is to submit to and respect her husband as the church does to Jesus.

The love God gives—an unconditional love that does anything to ensure our well-being, peace, joy—is seen in our husbands as they lay down their lives for us. And for a man to love his wife as he loves himself, he must share the highest level of trust, honesty, and respect with her.

The church submitting to Jesus is a picture of wives submitting to their husbands. To submit is to have "a voluntary attitude of giving in" to our husbands, "cooperating" with them, "assuming responsibility" with and for them, and "carrying" their "burden[s]."[5] True submission says, "I respect you and your God-given place of leadership in our home; therefore, I yield to your judgment, trusting that you will lead our family toward God's best for us."

Our marriages depend on our submission to and respect for our husbands as much as they depend on our husbands' love for us. God holds our husbands—the head of the home—ultimately responsible for the condition of our families. We need to recognize and respect their God-given role by cooperating with them, assuming responsibility with them, and carrying their burdens so that our families can continue toward the land of God's best for us. When we allow God's Word to guide our families, that is exactly where He will lead us.

Prayer

Father, in Jesus' name, I praise You for the gift of my husband. I ask You to lead me in my relationship with him so that I can bless him as the wife You desire for him. Father, I pray that You'll direct my husband and me in every area of our marriage so that we increasingly reflect the picture of Christ and the church. I choose to honor and obey Your Word, Lord. Amen.

The Help of the Holy Spirit

May the grace of the Lord Jesus Christ, and the love of God, and the fellowship of the Holy Spirit be with you all.

2 Corinthians 13:14 NIV

Today, our kids face all kinds of challenges in this world—peer pressure, rejection, and violence, just to name a few. As mothers today, we need something more than our five senses to keep our kids healthy and whole. We need help! Thank God, He has given us everything we need in the gift of the Holy Spirit, our Helper. Jesus said,

You...know how to give good gifts to your children. But your heavenly Father is even more ready to give the Holy Spirit to anyone who asks.

Luke 11:13 CEV

When we ask the Father for the gift of the Holy Spirit, He sends Him to dwell in us:

Do you not know that your body is the temple (the very sanctuary) of the Holy Spirit Who lives within you, Whom you have received [as a Gift] from God? You are not your own.

1 Corinthians 6:19 AMP

Life on the Go

When we moms fellowship with the Holy Spirit, we become sensitive to what He sees, hears, and knows about our children. The Bible offers many examples of how the Holy Spirit can help us, and we can apply each to our maternal responsibilities.

Acts 13:4 NIV says that Barabas and Paul were "sent on their way by the Holy Spirit." Just as the Holy Spirit sent Barabas and Paul on their ministry journey, He will help us direct our lives and the lives of our children. As we listen to His voice in our hearts, we will be able to help our children stay on His path for their lives.

As we fellowship with the Holy Spirit, He will also help us discern the integrity of the people around them. Acts 13:9 NIV tells us that Paul, "filled with the Holy Spirit," was able to discern and rebuke a man who was being motivated by the devil. Knowing what motivates a person will help us protect our children from those who would cause them harm.

When we spend time with the Holy Spirit, He will help us teach our children exactly what they need to know, when they need to know it. (See Acts 15:28 NIV.) When we rely on the Holy Spirit to train our children, they will understand and retain the knowledge we share with them.

As we instruct our children, the Holy Spirit will fill our mouths with His words. (See 2 Peter 1:21.) When we listen to the Holy Spirit, we can deliver a message straight from heaven to our children.

Perhaps the greatest benefit of knowing the Holy Spirit is having His help in praying for our kids:

> And the Holy Spirit helps us in our distress. For we don't even know what we should pray for, nor how we should pray. But the Holy Spirit prays for us with groanings that cannot be expressed in words.
>
> Romans 8:26 NLT

The Holy Spirit is our comforter, counselor, helper, intercessor, advocate, strengthener, and standby. (John 14:26 AMP.) He is a precious friend to us as mothers, and He wants to help us keep our kids healthy, whole, and prospering. When we give Him our lives, He can accomplish it all through us.

Take a Break

Listen for the voice of the Holy Spirit regarding each of your children, and follow His instructions.

Kick Out Guilt

Guilt is a motivator. If we allow it to, it can convince us to do some pretty foolish things. Sometimes our actions welcome guilt into our lives, but often it sneaks up on us without our ever realizing that it's completely out of place. A new mom may feel guilty for making time for herself away from her baby—even just to take a shower. Another mom may feel guilty for not being able to

> Let us draw near to God with a sincere heart in full assurance of faith, having our hearts sprinkled to cleanse us from a guilty conscience and having our bodies washed with pure water.
> Hebrews 10:19-22

give her child something that "all the other kids have." A working mom may feel guilty for not spending more time with her child. A stay-at-home mom may feel guilty for not helping make money for the family. Whatever the reason, many moms suffer from at least occasional bouts of guilt.

While guilt can lead us out of error and make us aware of a problem inside, it can't enable us to change. In fact, it often arrests our progress by blinding us to the solution—which is faith. Hebrews 10:19-22 tells us that through the blood of Jesus we can "draw near to God with a sincere heart in full assurance of faith, having our hearts sprinkled to cleanse us from a guilty conscience and having our bodies washed with pure water."

Guilt holds us in our prison of dissatisfaction with self, while faith directs us to the One who can cleanse us from guilt and lead us onward and upward. When we try to appease our guilt by ourselves, we often make mistakes, which lead to more guilt. But when our hearts are sprinkled clean from guilt, we gain God's perspective and make changes in His power.

Sure, we make mistakes, but the solution is not to wallow in guilt. The solution is Jesus:

> So now there is no condemnation for those who belong to Christ Jesus.
>
> Romans 8:1 NLT

When you make a mistake and guilt slaps you in the face, don't grab it and hold on to it to punish yourself. Let it go and reach with both hands for the One who can cleanse you and pull you up to the only expectation that truly matters—His own.

Prayer

Father, in Jesus' name, Your Word says that if we confess our sins, You are faithful and just to forgive us our sins. (1 John 1:9.) Lord, I repent for my sins, and I thank You that You do not condemn me. I put the past behind me, and I ask You to give me Your perspective of me. Help me walk in the victory over guilt that You've already won for me so that my only motivation in life is Your love, in Jesus' name. Amen.

A Grandmother's Love

> I have been reminded of your sincere faith, which first lived in your grandmother Lois and in your mother Eunice and, I am persuaded, now lives in you also.
>
> 2 Timothy 1:5

Through the lineage of Abraham, Isaac, Jacob, and all the way to Joseph and finally Jesus, we can see the value God places on family ties. And it's not so much the bloodline that matters: Mary conceived Jesus by the Holy Spirit, not by Joseph. What matters most is relationship.

A grandmother's relationship with God yields eternal fruit. Believing grandmothers have the opportunity to exemplify God's faithfulness and the blessing of a life spent with Him. The apostle Paul speaks of the treasure of such a grandmother in 2 Timothy 1:5: "I have been reminded of your sincere faith, which first lived in your grandmother Lois and in your mother Eunice and, I am persuaded, now lives in you also." What a blessed woman Lois was to impact the second and third generations with her personal faith, and how blessed Timothy was to benefit from her influence!

Through a grandmother, God can hand down great blessing and wisdom to the next generations. Whether she has walked with God her whole life or only recently come to know Him, a grandmother can speak into her children's and grandchildren's lives the priceless wisdom attained through personal experience. Titus speaks of the influence she can have when she is reverent in the way she lives and teaches what is good. (Titus 2:3.)

In the book of Ruth, we find a woman whose prayers, love, and godly influence impacted innumerable generations to follow. Through her loving influence with her widowed daugher-in-law, Naomi helped a union begin between Ruth and Boaz. As a result of their union, Naomi became the grandmother-in-love to Obed, whom she loved as her very own child. (Ruth 4:16.) Years later, her influence would reach King David, the grandson of Obed. Naomi's prayers and love yielding a worshipful shepherd-turned-king after God's own heart, the Great Shepherd, and ultimately all who would believe in Christ and become God's blood-bought sons and daughters.

As moms and grandmothers, we must never underestimate the profound and eternal impact we make on future generations every day. If we ask Him to, God will equip us with His wisdom to share with our children and grandchildren. Even if we cannot be with them, we can touch them with His love and influence—through our prayers.

for Moms

Take a Break

With a note, a phone call, or a prayer, reach out to your children and grandchildren with a personal touch of God's love today.

Know Him

God doesn't just want your warm body in the church building or your occasional prayer for a need or at the dinner table. He wants you. He wants to be closer to you than your heartbeat, and He wants you to know He is with you all the time. That is why He sent His Holy Spirit—so you could know His perpetual presence.

> Trust in the Lord with all thine heart; and lean not unto thine own understanding. In all thy ways acknowledge him, and he shall direct thy paths.
> Proverbs 3:5,6 KJV

The Holy Spirit confirms in your heart that God is your Father. (Rom. 5:5; Eph. 1:13.) He empowers you to do, to pray, and to speak God's will every day. (Acts 10:38; 1 Peter 1:21.) He comforts you and fills you with hope. (Rom. 15:13.) He teaches you. (Luke 12:12; John 14:26.) And He strengthens you with His joy. (Luke 10:21; Acts 13:52.)

Acknowledging God means knowing Him, perceiving Him, distinguishing Him from others, knowing Him by experience, recognizing Him, admitting and confessing that He is there, and considering His presence.[6] Whether you're doing the laundry, reading to your kids, or watching television, He wants you to be consciously aware of His presence.

When we are conscious of God's presence all day, every day, our behavior changes. We not only steer clear of sin, but we walk in step with God's victorious plan for our lives. He wants to lead us every moment in the way we should go. Then, as He leads us, we will train our kids by doing our jobs, loving our husbands, being good friends, and doing everything His way.

Just think. We have been given access to a personal assistant who will guide us perfectly every moment of every day. With Him, we can't go wrong. We can clean the house more efficiently than ever before; we can train our kids in a way that's custom-fit for each one of them; we can find true rest; and we can love others wholly. His name is Holy Spirit, and He guarantees our success in life—in truth, He guarantees life itself. (2 Cor. 1:21.)

Give the Lord your life by acknowledging His presence with you every day. He'll give you true life—abundantly.

Prayer

Father, I want to be Yours. I dedicate myself wholly to You. I lean on, trust in, and am confident in You in all my ways. Thank You that You direct my paths. Holy Spirit, be a part of every moment of my life, and lead me continually in Your ways. Thank You for Your anointing to walk Your path all of my days, in Jesus' name. Amen.

More

There is no limit to what God can do in and through and for you, and He has given you everything you need in this life and in the life to come in His Word. Salvation, healing, provision, peace, soundness—these words only begin to

> May the Lord make you increase, both you and your children.
> Psalm 115:14

describe what God wants to give you and will give you when you seek Him.

God has already given you everything you need. Now, the only thing left for you to do is receive it. When you start to dig into the truth of His Word, you'll discover that it is His endless treasure for you. You'll keep finding more wisdom, more encouragement, more joy, more forgiveness, more mercy, more strength—more of everything you could ever desire.

The more you find, the more you'll want. You'll echo the cry of the Psalmist, who said, "As the deer pants for streams of water, so my soul pants for you, O God" (Ps. 42:1). Inside you'll feel a deep hunger, and the only thing that will satisfy is Him. God wants you to seek Him daily—to read His Word, to listen to His Spirit, and to rest in Him—so He can satisfy your thirst and hunger with good things—with Him.

As you are filled with Him, you will be changed. You will decrease, and He will increase. In your weakness, He will be shown strong. Day by day, as you walk in His Spirit and not according to the flesh, you will become an increasingly clear reflection of God's glory:

> And we, who with unveiled faces all reflect the Lord's glory, are being transformed into his likeness with ever-increasing glory, which comes from the Lord, who is the Spirit.

> 2 Corinthians 3:18

God wants to complete you. He gave you the mirror of His Word to complete you. When you look into His mirror, you aim for completion in Him.

> Now we see but a poor reflection as in a mirror; then we shall see face to face. Now I know in part; then I shall know fully, even as I am fully known.

> 1 Corinthians 13:12

Give Him all you have—and get ready for more.

Prayer

Father, I want more of You. I love you with all my heart, with all my soul, and with all my strength. My entire being hungers and thirsts for nothing but You. Fill me, transform me, and use me for Your glory. Let me see You more clearly and reflect You more purely each day, in Jesus' name. Amen.

Give Them Everything

"Whoever accepts and trusts the Son gets in on every-thing, life complete and forever!"

John 3:36 MESSAGE

As moms, we want to give our kids everything they need. But more than anything else in life, our kids need Jesus. In fact, He is all they will ever need. His lordship guarantees abundant life, beginning on earth and extending into eternity.

In the beginning, humanity lived spiritually in communion with God. But when Adam sinned, we were separated from God and became spiritually dead. In order to reclaim His beloved creation, God sent Jesus. He laid down His life to give us His eternal life. At the cross, Jesus saw each of us and each of our children reuniting with the Father. That picture impelled Him to sacrifice everything for us.

Now we have the opportunity to receive His gift in our own lives and to share it with our children. We don't have to do anything to receive it, and we cannot earn it.

It is by grace you have been saved, through faith—and this not from yourselves, it is the gift of God—not by works, so that no one can boast.

Ephesians 2:8,9

God freely gave us the gift of salvation through His Son, and now we simply receive it by believing it and confessing it.

> The word is near you, in your mouth and in your heart (that is, the word of faith which we preach): that if you confess with your mouth the Lord Jesus and believe in your heart that God has raised Him from the dead, you will be saved. For with the heart one believes unto righteousness, and with the mouth confession is made unto salvation.

Romans 10:8-10 NKJV

To be saved, all we do is confess Jesus as Lord and believe in our hearts that God raised Him from the dead. To share the eternal gift of life with our kids, we simply need to tell them the Gospel message, then ask them if they believe and want to confess Jesus as Lord. It's as simple as saying, "Jesus is my Lord." When they do this, they will be completely changed spiritually. Second Corinthians 5:17 says that they become a new creation. Their spirits are reborn, and the Holy Spirit within them will confirm that God is their Father. (Gal. 4:6.)

Give your children the gift that will change them forever. Give them everything: Give them Jesus.

for Moms

Take a Break

Share the Gospel message with your children and give them the opportunity to say, "Jesus is my Lord."

Endnotes

[1] *Ask Dr. Sears,* "Seven Ways to Bond With Your Preborn Baby," http://www.askdrsears.com/html/1/T010608.asp.

[2] Easton, s.v. "yoke."

[3] 1 Timothy 5:9 NASB says, "A widow is to be put on the list only if…." According to Thayer's Greek-English Lexicon of the New Testament, this exclusive list was comprised "of those widows who held a prominent place in the church and exercised a certain superintendence over the rest of the women, and had charge of the widows and orphans supported at the public expense" (Thayer, s.v. *katalego,* Strong's #2639).

[4] Thayer, s.v. *timao,* Strong's #5091.

[5] Strong's #5293; *Hupotasso.*

[6] *Interlinear Study Bible,* http://www.studylight.org/isb/bible.cgi?query=pr+3%3A6&section=)
&it=nas&oq=pr%25203%3A6&ot=bhs&nt=na&new=1&nb=pr&ng=3&ncc=3>accessed September 2004, s.v. yada, Strong's #3045.

References

Ask Dr. Sears, http://www.askdrsears.com.

Easton, Mathew George. Easton's Bible Dictionary, http://www.studylight.org/dic/ebd/, 1897.

Strong, James. *Strong's Exhaustive Concordance of the Bible,* "Greek Dictionary of the New Testament" (Nashville: TN, Thomas Nelson Publishers, 1990.)

Thayer, Joseph H. *Thayer's Greek-English Lexicon of the New Testament,* Peabody, Massachusetts: Hendrickson Publishers, October 2003.

Prayer of Salvation

God loves you—no matter who you are, no matter what your past. God loves you so much that He gave His one and only begotten Son for you. The Bible tells us that "…whoever believes in him shall not perish but have eternal life" (John 3:16). Jesus laid down His life and rose again so that we could spend eternity with Him in heaven and experience His absolute best on earth. If you would like to receive Jesus into your life, say the following prayer out loud and mean it from your heart.

Heavenly Father, I come to You admitting that I am a sinner. Right now, I choose to turn away from sin, and I ask You to cleanse me of all unrighteousness. I believe that Your Son, Jesus, died on the cross to take away my sins. I also believe that He rose again from the dead so that I might be forgiven of my sins and made righteous through faith in Him. I call upon the name of Jesus Christ to be the Savior and Lord of my life. Jesus, I choose to follow You and ask that You fill me with the power of the Holy Spirit. I declare that right now I am

a child of God. I am free from sin and full of the right-
eousness of God. I am saved in Jesus' name. Amen.

If you prayed this prayer to receive Jesus Christ as
your Savior for the first time, please contact us on the Web
at **www.harrisonhouse.com** to receive a free book.

Or you may write to us at

Harrison House
PO Box 35035
Tulsa, Oklahoma 74153

Fishing Trips. Baseball Games. Late Nights at Work.

Fatherhood is a full-time job. There never seems to be enough hours in the day to "get it all done." Add in the desire to spend time with the heavenly Father and we realize that life is busy.

Let's face it—we live our lives "on the go." However, God wants us to experience true "life." Now you can take God's words of life wherever you go. The *Life on the Go Devotional for Dads* is packed full of meaningful devotionals, stories, Scriptures, humor, and prayers that will bring purpose and richness to your fast-paced life. Whether at the office, gym, or after the kids are in bed, prepare to become stronger by spending time with your heavenly "Dad."

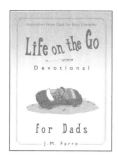

Life on the Go Devotional for Dads
1-57794-807-6

Available at bookstores everywhere
or visit **www.harrisonhouse.com**.

You've graduated and you're going out into the world. You are packing and leaving for the next big transition in your life. From classes and hanging out with your friends to interviews and work—it's a fast-paced world, and we are running a constant race of cell phones, computers, Web sites, magazines, coffee shops, meetings, late nights, and early mornings, all while trying to fit God in. But are we doing a good job?

Let's face it — we live our lives "on the go." However, God wants us to experience true "life." Now you can take God's words of life wherever you go. The *Life on the Go Devotional for Graduates* is packed full of meaningful devotionals and stories that will bring purpose and richness to your fast-paced life. Full of Scriptures, prayers, stories, and humor; you will be charged with these unique insights and encouragements from other grads that have "been there."

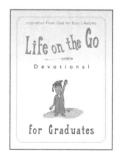

Life on the Go Devotional for Graduates
1-57794-806-8

Available at bookstores everywhere
or visit **www.harrisonhouse.com**.

www.harrisonhouse.com

Fast. Easy. Convenient!

◆ New Book Information

◆ Look Inside the Book

◆ Press Releases

◆ Bestsellers

◆ Free E-News

◆ Author Biographies

◆ Upcoming Books

◆ Share Your Testimony

◆ Online Product Availability

◆ Product Specials

◆ Order Online

For the latest in book news and author information, please visit us on the Web at www.harrisonhouse.com. Get up-to-date pictures and details on all our powerful and life-changing products. Sign up for our e-mail newsletter, *Friends of the House,* and receive free monthly information on our authors and products including testimonials, author announcements, and more!

Harrison House—
Books That Bring Hope, Books That Bring Change

The Harrison House Vision

Proclaiming the truth and the power
Of the Gospel of Jesus Christ
With excellence;

Challenging Christians to
Live victoriously,
Grow spiritually,
Know God intimately.